BEYOND THE BLUE

BEYOND THE BLUE

The Ultimate Insider's Look at the
First Decade of the XPRIZE Revolution

James Richard Campbell

Foreword by
Dr. Peter H. Diamandis, XPRIZE Founder

Kindred Spirit Press, Inc.
St. Augustine, Florida

Published by: Kindred Spirit Press, Inc., P.O. Box 3773, St. Augustine, FL 32085

Contact: 863-299-8680. publisher@aero-news.net

Printed in the United States of America

Editors: Jim Campbell, Nathan Cremisino, Eric Van Gilder, Shane Tully

Photographs © Jim Campbell

Cover design: Jim Campbell, Nathan Cremisino, Mayapriya Long (Bookwrights)

Text design by Mayapriya Long (Bookwrights)

Ebook Conversion(s): Bookwrights

ISBN Print Book: 978-1-886743-20-5

ISBN EBOOK MOBI: 978-1-886743-21-2

ISBN EBOOK EPUB: 978-1-886743-22-9

ISBN EBOOK APP: 978-1-886743-23-6

Beyond The Blue... A Dedication

To those of us fortunate to have seen Mother Earth from what many might consider to be a perilous (but otherwise soul-enriching) height, there is a barrier that one crosses on the way to where (I'm told) heaven resides.

As one climbs past the bulk of the Earth's atmosphere to exo-atmospheric altitudes; the warm greens, whites and blues of the ground, clouds and sky give way to a dark, colder, realm where much of the world is revealed—and what was once a vast tableau of seemingly flat terra firma takes on a curvature and expanse that is hard to absorb on first sight.

This transition... where you first start peering beyond much of our breathable atmosphere, I call 'Beyond The Blue'—and it is here that true adventure takes on a brilliant, if occasionally harsh, character that can and often will change how we view our world, our lives, and our very existence. I've also come to believe that no one should complete their lifespan without at least one such lofty glimpse—so as to gain perspective on how small we are—and how vast our potential truly remains.

XPRIZE and its many amazing offshoots, and

offspring, started changing the world well over a decade ago... not so much with the possibility that we might all, one day, get to go to space... but to allow us to build our lives with the firm knowledge that amazing things were possible if amazing dreams were dreamt... and pursued.

That, in a nutshell, is what this extraordinary decade taught me... and why, even now, the effect has been a stunning adjunct to a life lived on the edge... until I finally realized that that so-called edge was much farther out than I dared dream... until 2004.

As extraordinary as it was to record history, play with rockets, float for many many many hours in luscious Zero-G, to push boundary, after boundary, after boundary... it is the people of the XPRIZE revolution that empowered and impressed me most of all. And it is, first and foremost, that I dedicate this work to them... my co-conspirators, fellow flyers, adventure partners, and an endless source of inspiration, strength and (yes) amusement.

To Peter Diamandis and Gregg Maryniak... who not only changed the world, but demonstrated time and time again that friendship was more than a forgotten concept (or worse, a much-abused phrase),

but a privilege and an honor—and who challenged me beyond measure—my thanks. Always.

Folks, I'm not a follower… never have been… but these are two guys that I will follow to the ends of the earth… and far beyond. With glee.

And yet there were so many other incredible friendships that became a foundation of my XPRIZE experience… especially my work with Ian Murphy, one of the best PR experts I've ever met and a surprisingly down to Earth fellow -- for a space guy. His Mother, Diane, is responsible for many of the most pivotal successes of the early and continuing XPRIZE outreach efforts—and is about as classy as any person gets.

And then there is Anousheh Ansari… while she and her family put up the big bucks that allowed XPRIZE to pay up when history was made, it has been her gentle and yet determined guidance that may have been her greatest gift (of all) to the XP movement. Personally, though, I remember a wondrous conversation we had, while she was onboard the International Space Station and I was on the ground (no—not my preferred placement), in which we discussed her wonder with her surroundings and the peace she felt whilst looking down at the rest of us on the Big Blue Marble. Of all the discussions I've ever had in my life and with so many astonishing people,

it stands out as one of the most profound. What an amazing lady!

And then there is the XPRIZE crew itself… hundreds of people who shared an uncommon vision of things quite possible to those with a common goal. There were hundreds of them… and they occupy my fondest memories, and are often a part of my favorite stories… and boy, did we have fun!

To all my many friends and fellow flyers from the Zero-Gravity experience… both the staff and flyers that made this project possible, as well as all those who allowed me to watch their first tenuous experience with something that they had only barely imagined. The smiles that erupted from all those first-time flyers are some of the best memories in my collection… and it was a joy to share them.

The Rocket Racing League was, ultimately and unfortunately, not yet a success… for now. Running out of the Bucks one needs these days to play Buck Rogers, the RRL experience and my being named as one of the Four Founding Pilots along with my friends Rick Searfoss, Sean Tucker and Erik Lindbergh, was none-the-less a great source of pride and a true challenge. But mark my words, someday it will blast off once again… bigger, better, faster and higher than ever before… and when it does, I plan to be there. This is one Rocket Pilot that is ready, willing and able to saddle up and push the boundaries, with such visionary spirits, whenever and wherever they're ready. It is because of this project that I came into contact with even more exceptional people and flyers… including the ever-empowering Granger Whitelaw, Jeff Greason, and so many others that look for new boundaries… so that they can push past them. WAY past them.

And along the way, there have been some amazing men and women… people who have demanded much from me, inspired me and made me a better person in so many ways… my grandfather Dr. Morris Schwartz, EAA Founder Paul Poberezny, Cirrus Founder Alan Klapmeier, retired AOPA President Phil Boyer and, of course, so many others.

I've endeavored to master the photographic arts all my life, starting with the tutelage of the National Geographic Society's Chuck O'Rear—who was the first to put a Pro camera in my hands for them. His solid advice has allowed me to take some of the most stunning photographs of the nascent commercial space race. I'd be remiss if I didn't also commend and thank Randy Leffingwell, for his wise counsel, friendship and the superlative work that has so inspired me.

To my staff, partners and associates… the talented men and women who put up with me as they helped me create the Aero-News Network, Aero-TV, Airborne, Kindred Spirit Press, nearly 200,000 published stories, over 8000 podcasts, some 2000 Aero-TV programs, over 20 books and more adventures (and misadventures) than I can count… you have my gratitude and respect for putting up with me and allowing us to achieve so much because of your tremendous skills, vast creativity, and incredible patience. Nathan, Ashley, Earl, Eric, John, Juan, Birgit, and so many others… thank you…

I am the first of seven kids in a dynamic family that defies true explanation. They have provided the foundation for every great thing I have ever done and helped me pick myself back up from every dumb stunt I've ever recovered from. Inexplicably; they put up with me…but I suspect they do so for the shear entertainment value of watching what crazy thing I'm going to do next. They are proof positive that the genetic lottery was kind to me.

I once loved a brilliant and lovely little girl that I was privileged to show how amazing the world of flight could be… and after a first date that included an aerobatic flight that ignited a passion for unlimited aerobatics that took her to the very heights of the sport aviation world and many a championship, I married Vicki and thought my life was complete. But life takes strange, even unwelcome, turns. God had other plans… and our rocky road ended abruptly with her death at the World Aerobatic Championships 5 years ago. I've mollified the pain of her loss with the belief that God needed an Angel more than I needed my best and forever friend… and I pray that this lovely girl has found the heaven my heart knows she deserves…

And then there is the ultimate proof that all lives have limitless possibilities—many of which we'd never even considered. This one took the form of a cute, shy, and subtly expressive soul who became a friend—then my best friend—teaching me that life and love are limitless in scope and potential… and proved it by helping me to 'ruin' a perfectly good friendship with a new and altogether unexpected love, several years ago, that has become the focal point of my life.

I am, without doubt, incredibly blessed…and now my life is dedicated to much more than the next adventure, but also the life I am building with my buddy, friend, wife and partner at my side.

Masako… you are the greatest adventure of all…

Beyond The Blue!

Jim Campbell, 01.09.14
St. Augustine, FL, USA, Planet Earth
(Third Planet Out From SOL… you can't miss it)

CONTENTS

The Ansari XPRIZE:
Reflections 10 Years Later

By Peter H. Diamandis, MD

It's a pleasure to write this foreword because it's the first time that I'm actually getting to tell the story of the founding of XPRIZE and the creation of the Ansari XPRIZE. It's hard to believe that it's been 10 years since Mike Melvill and Brian Binnie flew SpaceShipOne to 100 kilometers altitude within a five-day span to win the $10 million Ansari XPRIZE. And even more startling, it's been 20 years since I came up with the idea of the XPRIZE.

My passion for space began early. I was born in May 1961, both the year and month that President John F. Kennedy announced America's mission to the Moon. While I wasn't conscious of it at the time, the sequence of events that his vision ignited had a profound effect on my life. The release of the Star Trek TV series in 1967 and the Apollo Moon landings shaped me, and helped inspire my life's passion and purpose, the desire to be a space explorer and someone who helped facilitate humanity's journey beyond the Earth. Not something that was typically discussed around the house.

My parents were both born on the island of Lesvos in Greece. They grew up in small villages and eventually immigrated to the United States. My father was an obstetrician and gynecologist and my mom ran his office. Early on, it was expected that I would become a physician, and take over my father's practice. But, I had other plans. My interest in space filled my dreams and drove my aspirations.

When I finally got to college at MIT, I studied molecular biology and a pre-med curriculum by day, and focused on my personal passion for space at night and on weekends. There, I founded Students for the Exploration and Development of Space (SEDS) and then later on with Todd Hawley and Bob Richards, co-founded the International Space University (ISU). It was through SEDS and ISU that I first met Gregg Maryniak. It was Gregg Maryniak, who in 1993, gave me a copy of The Spirit of St. Louis. His purpose in giving me the book was to inspire me to complete my pilot's license, which, due to the demands of my

1

medical school program, I'd started and abandoned twice since meeting him.

When I read *The Spirit of St. Louis*, I was taken by Lindbergh's story and amazed by the $25,000 Orteig prize that inspired him to cross the Atlantic. Before reading this book I had no idea that there was a prize involved. I assumed that one day Lindbergh took off from New York and crossed the Atlantic. Raymond Orteig was born in France and came to the United States at the turn of the 1900s. While he started his life here nearly penniless, he quickly worked his way up from a busboy, to hotel manager and eventually to owner of the Hotel Lafayette. During World War 1, he befriended many of the young 'aviators' who stayed at his hotel who told him stories of their daring aerial adventures. Inspired by the potential of aviation, in 1919 he offered up a $25,000 prize for the first person to fly between New York and Paris.

As I read Lindbergh's story, I made notes in the margin. I was amazed by how much money the teams were spending to win $25,000, some as much as $100,000. I remember totaling it up at the end, and being astonished that it was nearly $400,000 or 16 times the prize purse. Equally incredible, was the fact that Lindbergh appeared to be the least qualified guy to win the competition given his short flying career at the time. I was fascinated by the idea, that by offering up an incentive competition, Orteig had automatically backed a winner.

I thought about Orteig's prize and the implications.

A $25,000 purse commanded $400,000 in team expenditures and ultimately gave birth to today's multi-hundred billion-dollar aviation industry. Lindbergh himself raised a total of about $20,000 from a group of St. Louisans to develop his airplane. The group that backed him called themselves "The Spirit of St. Louis Organization" and Lindbergh named his airplane after them.

As I finished reading Lindbergh's book, I started thinking about a prize to promote spaceflight and wrote down in the margin "XPRIZE???". My thinking at the time was that perhaps a prize could be used to develop private spaceships for the rest of us. I had long since given up on the idea that I would actually travel to space as a government astronaut, and if I could create a prize to encourage the creation of a new generation of private spaceships, perhaps that would be my ticket to space. Since I had no idea who would be my title sponsor, or my 'Orteig', I used 'x' as a place holder, and thus the origin of the name XPRIZE. 'X' was meant as a variable to be replaced by the name of the prize donor like the Orteig Prize or Nobel Prize.

A few months later I wrote up my XPRIZE idea and shared it with a few people. Jim Burke of the Jet Propulsion Lab and Gregg Maryniak of the Space Studies Institute were among the first to see the concept. I then wrote an article that appeared in the National Space Society magazine and was invited to give testimony in Congress about it.

The year was 1994.

It was during this testimony that I first met Doug King. At that time, Doug was the president of the Challenger Centers. A few months later he was recruited to St. Louis to become the president of the St. Louis Science Center. One evening, over dinner, we started discussing XPRIZE.

Doug said, "You have to come to St. Louis. St. Louis is where you'll find the funds to support this vision".

Once the fourth largest city in the United States, St. Louis had descended to number 40, and was eager to regain its reputation as an aerospace leader. So, with an invitation from Doug and with my good friend Gregg Maryniak, now as my partner, we traveled to St. Louis and met the one person that Doug believed could raise the capital.

His name was Alfred Kerth.

Al, as we knew him, was one of the great thinkers and promoters of St. Louis and in my first meeting with him he got so excited he stood up and shouted: "I get it. I get it. Let's make this happen."

We met that evening at the Racquet Club for scotch and he laid out his vision. We would create the NEW Spirit of St. Louis organization that would follow in the footsteps of the original. The New Spirit of St. Louis (NSSL) would be a group of 100 St. Louisans who contribute $25,000 each to provide the seed capital to launch XPRIZE.

On March 4th of 1996, we held another meeting at the Racquet Club, at the same table where Lindbergh himself had raised his original $20,000. That evening we raised about $500,000 from 20 St. Louisans who pledged to join NSSL. First to sign was Ralph Korte whose enthusiasm for the NSSL concept helped encourage Kerth to propose it. Also early to sign was my friend and business partner Marc Arnold, along with St. Louis leaders: Richard Fleming, John F. McDonnell, Dr. William H. Danforth, Hugh Scott, III, Andrew Taylor, Lotsie Holton and Walter Metcalfe, Jr. About two months later, in mid-May, we used that seed funding to boldly announce the $10 million prize competition, albeit without actually having the $10 million in place.

On May 18th, 1996, under the St. Louis arch with Al Kerth, Gregg Maryniak, and (now) Robert K. Weiss as thought partners, we held a major press conference announcing our intention to run a $10 million dollar competition for the first team who could build and fly a spaceship carrying three adults to 100 kilometers altitude twice within two weeks.

On the stage under the arch, we had not one astronaut, but 20, organized by my good friends, early XPRIZE co-founder Byron Lichtenberg and Colette Bevis. Chief among the astronauts was Apollo astronaut, and my hero, Buzz Aldrin. Also on stage with us, were Dan Goldin the NASA Administrator,

and Patti Grace Smith, the Associate Administrator of the FAA, as well as Erik and Morgan Lindbergh, the grandsons of Charles Lindbergh, and finally last, but not least, aviation legend Burt Rutan.

That day, hundreds of press reported on the story and gave birth to the idea of the XPRIZE above the line of super credibility. People got it; people believed it and it was a brilliant launch. That same evening, May 18th, we held a black tie gala dinner at the St. Louis Science Center and one of our guest speakers, Burt Rutan, took that opportunity to announce his intention to compete, formally becoming our first contender. His words were powerful and prophetic.

"I have never been as creative, eyeballing this god-damn prize," said Rutan, wearing his tuxedo. "I'm not going to tell you what I've come up with, because I want to win this thing!"

With the competition effectively launched, and no money in the bank, the hard work was just beginning —the work to fund not only the $10 million purse, but also the operation of the foundation itself. In partnership with Gregg Maryniak, Colette Bevis, and Byron Lichtenberg, I set out hat in hand to raise the capital. As bullish as I was, pitch after pitch failed to turn up a title sponsor. I presented to well over 150 CEOs, CMOs and philanthropists, everyone from Fred Smith of FedEx to Richard Branson of the Virgin Group, but the audacity of the prize and the chance that someone could die in the attempt, stalled our search for a sponsor.

The New Spirit of St. Louis Organization added members slowly, $25,000 at a time, and it was those funds that allowed us to continue operations. At our annual dinner in 1997, Tom Clancy was our guest speaker and while he was on stage, he announced that he wanted to join the New Spirit of St. Louis Organization, and better still, he wanted to buy four memberships. That announcement gathered significant press and generated an article in the Boston Globe. A week later I was contacted by First

USA Credit Card, which heard about the XPRIZE, and wanted to create a vanity credit card to help us raise money.

These funds helped us continue along but ultimately were not enough to fund the purse. It was then that two friends of mine told me about the idea of a 'hole-in-one insurance policy', the notion that one could buy an insurance policy to underwrite the prize. Here is the way it works. We had to set an end date to the competition. We selected December 31st, 2004. We would buy an insurance policy and pay a multimillion dollar premium. If someone were to win the prize by making the two flights to space within two weeks before that deadline, then the insurance policy would pay the $10 million dollars. If no one pulled it off, then the insurance company would keep the premiums. We were basically placing a large Las Vegas bet.

I turned to two friends, Bruce Kraselsky and Jean Michel Eid, to purchase the insurance. Ultimately, the insurance policy cost us about $3 million. The insurance underwriter hired a consultant to evaluate all the teams registered for the competition. They approached companies like Orbital Sciences, Lockheed and Boeing only to verify that they did not intend to compete. The big players were somewhat dismissive of the idea that a start-up entrepreneur could build a private spaceship and fly to space.

Luckily the insurance underwriter took the bet.

All I had to do now was come up with a three million dollar premium payment. The problem was that I didn't have $3 million. What I did instead was negotiate with the insurance company for a series of progress payments. The XPRIZE would make a $50,000 payment every month for a year, and then make a $2.6 million dollar balloon payment at the end of one year. The insurance underwriter was effectively giving us runway to raise the funds. Their expectation was that they would collect the premium and never pay out.

The first couple of $50,000 payments we made from funds we had raised. I made one payment personally, and then we were out of money. Every month Gregg and I would need to go and raise the money. It was not an easy task. I remember many Monday mornings looking at just five days to raise $50,000, or the competition was over. We made many new friends and many of our board members, folks like Adeo Ressi, Barry Thompson, Jack Bader and others, helped underwrite those '$50,000 Fridays'.

The next challenge: raising a rapidly approaching $2.6 million dollar balloon payment. It was at this point that I met my guardian angel, who came to me in the form of a Fortune magazine article. I was in my Santa Monica apartment on a Saturday afternoon, catching up on some reading when I flipped thru a copy of a Fortune magazine issue featuring the 'wealthiest women under 40'. One of those women was named Anousheh Ansari, and as I read her write-up, I stopped dead in my tracks and read it over and over again.

"It is my dream to fly on a sub-orbital flight into space," said Ms. Ansari.

Anousheh, like me, had grown up dreaming about Star Trek and becoming a space explorer. As I read further, I learned that Anousheh, her husband Hamid, and brother-in-law Amir Ansari had just sold their third company called Telecom Technologies to Sonus Networks for over a billion dollars. I knew in that moment, after five years of searching, that I had found our sponsor. The year was 2001, just before the meltdown.

When I tried to track Anousheh and Hamid down, I learned that she had been on vacation for two months in Hawaii following the sale of their company. I tracked down Anousheh's past executive secretary and extracted a solemn promise from her that if I sent her a FedEx package of materials on the XPRIZE, she would forward it to Anousheh in Hawaii. A week later I received a message back that Anousheh would meet with me in their Dallas offices. I asked Byron Lichtenberg to join me for the meeting. Byron and I flew down to Dallas to meet Anousheh, Hamid and Amir. We presented the XPRIZE vision and expressed our great desire to have them underwrite the purse and the operations of our first prize.

Little did I know that, according to Anousheh, they were sold within the first 10 minutes. I waited two days to hear from Hamid who called to say yes, that they would do it, that they would fund the operations and fund the remaining insurance payments. Shortly thereafter we announced the purse had been fully funded, and was now being re-named the Ansari XPRIZE, in their honor. Now, the only question was, could anybody win this before the December 31st, 2004 deadline?

Over the course of the competition, 26 different teams from seven countries entered to compete. I remember that in the early days Gregg Maryniak, Byron Lichtenberg and I would ponder how would we win this competition if we were competing. We each had our favorite design for getting three passengers to 100 kilometers: liquid engines, hybrid engines or solid engines; a helicopter first stage, balloon first stage, towed behind a plane, carried under or over a plane, vertical takeoff, horizontal takeoff; landing on land or landing in the water. During the course of the competition, every design was explored by one team or another. The competition was almost Darwinian in the breadth of the experimentation that took place.

Another fond memory of mine took place in 2003. A year before the prize was to be awarded. In a meeting with Marion Blakey, the FAA administrator, and Patti Smith the associate administrator, I explained how the current FAA rules did not allow for private spaceflight. In order for the competition to be won in the U.S., the rules would have to changed, or teams would need to fly from outside U.S. territories.

In her southern drawl the Administrator responded with: "Well then, we'll just have to change the rules, won't we?"

True to her word, she worked with Patti Smith to write regulations that ultimately allowed for private spaceflight to blossom.

Six months before the looming December 31st, 2004 deadline, Burt Rutan gave the XPRIZE official notice of his intention to fly. Rutan's first flight would take place on June 21st, 2004 as a systems test flight, and while it would attempt to get to the full XPRIZE altitude of 100 kilometers it would not be carrying the full weight load of three passengers. With Mike Melvill, perhaps Scaled Composite's most seasoned pilot at the controls, the flight was a success. We called this flight 'X-Zero', and dubbed the two official qualifying flights required to win the $10 million 'X1' and 'X2'.

On June 21st, the world watched as SpaceShipOne, powered by a hybrid engine burning nitrous oxide (laughing gas) and polybutadiene (tire rubber) took flight. The vehicle made it to space, just barely

clearing the 100-kilometer altitude target by a few hundred meters. This flight represented the first time a private vehicle had flown a single individual into space. It also cleared the way for Burt to give notice for other XPRIZE flights. Those flights took place on September 29th for X1. In keeping with his usual fanfare, Rutan chose October 4th to conduct X2, a date that represented the anniversary of USSR's launch of Sputnik, the first satellite ever to fly into space launched in 1957. Also on June 21st, Paul Allen, Microsoft co-founder and billionaire philanthropist was announced to be the official financial backer of the SpaceShipOne development project.

It's hard to fathom how much work went into reaching the October 4th 2004 milestone. That day has been, and always will be, a special day for me. I remember leaving my Santa Monica apartment at 2:00 AM and driving 2 hours out to the Mojave Desert to meet up with my team. Through the night, tens of thousands of people descended from around the world to be there for the historic event. With me that day were my mom and dad, my girlfriend (soon to be wife), Kristen and all of my closest friends. Under the guidance of Robert Weiss, Dan Pallotta (our producer) and Stuart Witt (Manager of the Mojave Air and Spaceport), we spent a huge amount of money to host all the aerospace VIPs, fans and media. What I remember most vividly besides the ocean of people who had gathered, was the lineup of close to one hundred satellite news trucks camped out to watch and see whether Burt Rutan and Paul Allen could win the $10 million Ansari XPRIZE.

In the pre-dawn hours, the carrier airplane, WhiteKnightOne, was being fuelled and SpaceShipOne was being readied. The pilot on this X2 flight was Navy fighter pilot and SpaceShipOne test pilot Brian Binnie.

Brian would go on to become our Charles Lindbergh.

A tall, thin man with a generous attitude and a strong supporter of XPRIZE over the years, we could imagine no one better to carry the torch of commercial space on that day. The story of his piloting the winning flight that day is a great one worth telling, but one that I will leave to him to recount.

To help tell our own story that morning, we set up an entire TV studio to webcast the competition live. I remember being on stage when SpaceShipOne, suspended under WhiteKnightOne, rolled down the long runway, the crowd applauding wildly. One person was waiving a sign "NASA Zero—SpaceShip One". By my side, on stage, was Stuart Witt, a dear friend and wonderful entrepreneur who made that day possible with his can-do attitude. Following the successful SS1 flights, Witt went on to take the airport to great fame and business success.

Just after sunrise, WhiteKnightOne's twin Williams FJ44 jet engines carried SpaceShipOne from the Earth's surface on an hour-long ascent to 60,000 feet. Our high-magnification TV cameras watched from the ground and broadcast the image to both the TV stations and large Jumbotron screens for the crowd to see. Edwards Air Force Base, a mere 50 miles away, watched the spaceship's flight on its radar, helping us measure its exact altitude to determine if we had a winner.

It was a magical moment when Brian's voice boomed out over the loudspeakers "Release, release, release." Seconds later SpaceShipOne was released from WhiteKnightOne, then a few seconds later, its hybrid engine ignited and Brian was thrown back into his seat as multiple Gs hurled the ship upwards towards space. Brian flew a picture perfect flight. The vehicle not only exceeded the 100 kilometers required to win the $10 million but shattered the X15 altitude record set some 40 years earlier.

Upon landing, Brian was surrounded by friends and family, he then stood atop SpaceShipOne draped in a U.S. Flag—a proud patriot grateful that such a venture could be funded, build and flown privately in the U.S. Brian later joined me on stage to capture and celebrate the winning moment. Along with me, were Anousheh and Amir Ansari, the benefactors of the Ansari XPRIZE, and Paul Allen, the visionary investor who backed Burt Rutan with some $25 million of capital to build SpaceShipOne. Next to Paul was Burt Rutan, next to Burt was Brian Binnie, and next to Brian was mega-entrepreneur Sir Richard Branson, who as it turned out, had recently negotiated the right to purchase the rights to SpaceShipOne in order to create a follow-on commercial vehicle, SpaceShipTwo for Virgin Galactic.

I first learned of Richard's deal the week before X1, when I first saw the red Virgin logo emblazoned on the tail of SpaceShipOne along-side the XPRIZE logo. Despite being somewhat peeved that Richard had turned me down twice over the years for funding the $10 million purse (first through Virgin Atlantic, and again through Virgin Mobile), in retrospect, I'm glad he opted instead to fund the development of the winning technology. After the successful X1 and X2 flights, the Virgin Group committed a quarter of a billion dollars to develop SpaceShipTwo. We had long-since hoped that the Ansari XPRIZE would lead to commercial space travel, we just didn't expect to have it happen during the actual competition. Richard very graciously gave me a ticket to fly on an early Virgin Galactic flight to space, allowing me to fulfill my personal dream of spaceflight. Having my XPRIZE efforts lead directly to the fulfillment of my childhood dreams is something I liken to the concept to throwing myself a touch-down pass.

Another vivid October 4th memory was having the XPRIZE capture the coveted Google Doodle real estate. On the Google homepage, soon after the winning flight was completed, was an image of SpaceShipOne flying over the Google logo, next to it a small flying saucer with two green aliens observing the flight. That Google Doodle later lead to my addressing a room full of 4,000 Googlers at the Googleplex on the Ansari XPRIZE, and a subsequent lunch with Larry Page, Google co-founder (then co-President and now CEO).

During that lunch I presented an impromptu invitation for him to join the XPRIZE Board of Trustees (which he happily accepted). His participation, along with Sergey Brin, Eric Schmidt, Wendy Schmidt, Elon Musk, Jim Gianopulos, Arianna Huffington, James Cameron and other notable figures who subsequently joined the XPRIZE Board of Trustees breathed new life (and capital) into XPRIZE, fueling our commitment to use prizes to take on the world's grand challenges and create large-scale incentive competitions where market failures existed.

Since that time XPRIZE has expanded.

We are now designing, building and launching prizes in five areas: (i) exploration (ocean and space), (ii) health and life sciences, (iii) energy and the environment, (iv) global development and (v) learning. Wherever we find a great market failure in need of innovation, we do our best to marry-up a clear and measurable objective, and a benefactor or corporate sponsor to launch an XPRIZE.

Since our first prize launch, the Ansari XPRIZE, I'm proud to report we've launched the $10M Progressive Insurance Automotive XPRIZE, the $30M Google Lunar XPRIZE, the $2M Northrop Grumman Lunar Lander XChallenge, the $1.4M Wendy Schmidt Ocean Cleanup X Challenge, the $10M Qualcomm Tricorder XPRIZE, the $2.4M Nokia Sensing X Challenge and most recently the $2M Wendy Schmidt Ocean Health XPRIZE.

We are entering a point in history where entrepreneurs are now capable of doing what only the largest companies and governments could only do before. Forty years ago, only a government could build a spaceship. Today, a small team of 30 engineers powered by exponential technologies, can build a ship that travels into space. In the same way that I believe that there is no problem that cannot be solved, that entrepreneurs powered by technology can take on any challenge and find a solution, I believe that we've entered a day and age where we can stop complaining about problems and start solving them.

Today, when you go to the Smithsonian and look up from the central foyer, you see the Spirit of St. Louis airplane and right next to it, above the Apollo 11 capsule, is SpaceShipOne. Seventy-seven years after Lindbergh's famous flight, driven by Raymond Orteig's passion and vision, the first private space flights took place.

I wonder what SpaceShipOne and the Ansari XPRIZE will inspire in the year 2081, seventy-seven years after the winning flights?

A special think you to Jim Campbell for photographing the entire journey between X-Zero to X-1, and for the creation of this beautiful book. Without his effort this story would not be properly told.

For those of you who supported XPRIZE over this last 20 years, you have my personal thanks.

To those of you new to this story, I ask: What do you prize?

What challenge do you want to solve?

We've entered a new era, one in which the world's biggest problems are the world's biggest market opportunities. One in which, I believe there is no challenge that cannot be solved.

Best wishes, and see you in space,

Peter H. Diamandis, MD
Founder, Chairman & CEO, XPRIZE Foundation

New Spirit Of St. Louis Organization

"With every day that passes here in New York, I realize more fully that, aside from a plane with performance enough to make the flight, my greatest asset lies in the character of my partners in St. Louis."

—Excerpt from *The Spirit of St. Louis* by Charles Lindbergh, the book that spurred the creation of the XPRIZE

In 1996, our brilliant and greatly missed friend, Al Kerth, suggested that the entrepreneurial spirit of St. Louis could once again propel America to the forefront of aviation by supporting a prize to create a completely new private space industry. Imagine going to potential backers in the late 1990's and saying "Back us with $25,000, and we'll make private spaceships happen."

But that is exactly what Al Kerth, Peter Diamandis and I did. St. Louis (and many honorary St. Louisans) came through… and the rest is history, with *SpaceShipOne* hanging next to the *Spirit of St. Louis* in the National Air and Space Museum, private spacecraft now delivering supplies to the International Space Station and firms offering the first suborbital commercial space flights.

The following members of the New Spirit of St. Louis Organization are directly responsible for changing the way the world views spaceflight through their support of XPRIZE in the beginning. In addition to igniting the private spaceflight revolution, they made possible the modern renaissance of incentive prizes that are addressing the Grand Challenges of our time and providing hope for tomorrow.

All of us at the XPRIZE thank and salute these courageous souls who made the dreams depicted in these pages come true.

Gregg Maryniak
Director and Secretary, XPRIZE

Douglas Albrecht; Anne Albrecht; Paul Allen; Amir Ansari; Anousheh Ansari; Marc Arnold; Ronald L. Atkinson; Anne H. Bader; Jack G. Bader; David & Karen Bayer; Andrew Beal; Donna Beck; Brian Binnie; Dan & Gloria Bohan; Alan B. Bornstein; John & Tammy Browning; Ralph Buffano; Charles E. Claggett, Jr.; Tom Clancy; Jerry Clinton; Bert & Karen Condie, honoring H.L. Giesler; William H. Danforth; Dr. John F. Demartini; Dr. Peter Diamandis; Harry P. Diamandis; Richard C.D. Fleming; Sam Fox; Michael E. Gaddis, Garrett Gruener and Amy Slater; Richard A. Garriott; Ron Henges; Tom Hesterman; Jack Hidary; Jean & Wells Hobler; William.F. and Kerry Holekamp; Lotsie Hermann Holton; Bill Huang; William James Foundation; Richard & Susan Kane; Alfred H. Kerth III; Douglas R. King; John & Martha King; Walter Kistler; John E. and Susan Klein; Ralph Korte; E. Desmond Lee; Mary Ann Lee; Richard A. Leeds; Erik Lindbergh; Robert Lorsch; William E. Maritz; John & Adrienne Mars; Gregg Maryniak; Brian L. Matthews; Carol D. Matthews; Margie Wolcott May; John F. McDonnell; Michael McDowell; Dennis & Grace McGillicuddy; Mike Melvill; Walter L. Metcalfe, Jr.; Orville J. Middendorf; Dan & Carolyn Miller; Elon Musk; Kimbal & Jennifer Musk; Ralph & Phyllis Nansen; Carmelo Natoli; Cark H. Novotny & Judith L. Swahnberg; Stewart D. Nozette; William Orthwein; Dan Pallotta; Harry & Stella Pappas; Michael Perusse for Michael, Allison and Regan; Peter Preuss; Adeo Ressi Di Cervia; Glenda & Jim Rice; Patricia Rodeheaver; Donald l. Ross; Richard Rubenstein; Burt Rutan; Dennis L. Ryll; Robert & Janet Sabes Foundation; Steven F. Schankman; Hugh Scott III; Ghassan Shaker; Barry and Trudy Silverstein; Brice R. Smith III; Holly D. Smith; Holly P. Smith; Jessamine, Katlin, McKall, Bordon & Hattie Smith; Tom & Maurie Smith; John & Michelle Socha-Leialoha; Michael Staenberg; John M. Stephens; Steven J. Stogel; Dr. Richard Sugden; Richard T. Sullivan; Andrew C. Taylor; Barbara B. Taylor; Karen & Francis Taylor IV; J. Barry Thompson; Erik & Stephanie Tilenius; David Treinis; Steve & Michelle Trulaske; George Von Hoffman, Jr.; Robert K. Weiss; Lisa Wendt; Richard White; Granger Whitelaw; Simon Peter Worden; Irving P. Zuckerman.

Ansari XPRIZE Sponsors

Title Sponsor:
The Ansari Family

Presenting Sponsor:
Champ Car World Series

Additional Sponsors:
7UP, M&M Mars,
The New Spirit of St. Louis Organization,
St. Louis Science Center

One Wild Ride: Peter, Gregg And The Whole Insanely Magnificent Adventure That Gave Me A Ringside Seat To History—And Beyond

While the tale I will tell, and the images that I present, belong to history and the world, they have a far more personal meaning (and value) to me.

With the Tenth Anniversary of the amazing victory that took place with the winning of the Ansari XPRIZE now approaching, I'm a little flabbergasted to catalog all that has occurred in the time since a pivotal meeting in Oshkosh, WI... and all that might yet be accomplished in the future.

And before I get too far into this tale, let me explain the way that I've told this story. I play many a role in my life. As a test pilot, I produce highly detailed, clinical reports about the issues and flight test exercises that I am called upon to write. As an aviation journalist, I am called upon to write clear, understandable narratives about the facts of a story and to clearly distinguish the difference between what is news and what is editorial opinion or analysis. But... as the principal photographer, author and

historian for much of the First Decade of the XPRIZE revolution, I decided to veer far away from much of that to ALSO communicate the joy, enthusiasm, genius, and the occasional insanity, that became my treasured moments with all things XPRIZE...

It may be a little jarring, somewhat informal, even irreverent, and a little over-the-top now and then... but this is the XPRIZE decade I lived and loved... with none of the boundless joy and endless wonder held back.

With luck, you'll get a feel for the intensity of it all... and the extraordinary human and technical moments that changed the world.

On to our tale...

Sometime over a decade ago, a growing friendship with a fellow by the name of Gregg Maryniak started a cascade of events, including another friendship with the irrepressible Peter Diamandis, the founder of the XPRIZE, which has given me some of the most indelible memories of my life.

And that's saying a lot… I've been a test pilot, commercial pilot, skydiver, airshow pilot, aviation journalist, writer, photographer and been selected as a founding pilot for one of the most exciting rocket programs ever imagined—and a lot of other things involved in the aviation world for all my adult life… and never have I wanted much for adventure… but what came my way via the XPRIZE revolution, and its many unique offspring, still floors me to this day.

The escalation of my life into the XPRIZE world started with an introduction by Gregg to Peter, suitably enough, at the annual Oshkosh EAA AirVenture Fly-In and Convention, the largest aviation gathering of its type in the world. A simple meeting turned into a fascinating conversation—ideas flowed, plans were made, and within weeks I was well-ensconced on a whirlwind of adventures, initiatives, wonders and global game-changers… in short, everyday XPRIZE stuff.

XPRIZE was brilliantly futuristic… and yet it started with a simple bit of history.

The XPRIZE project was more than a $10 Million Dollar prize to open up the private/commercial space tourism industry—it was the impetus behind many affiliated programs and offshoots that rocked the public's comprehension about what might and might not be possible in their lifetimes.

It was based on a devilishly simple concept… one with an impeccable historical precedent… and one with a comparable effect on the world at the time. In 1919, New York hotel owner Raymond Orteig offered a $25,000 prize to the first pilot flying non-stop from New York City to Paris or vice-versa.

The offer was made in a letter to Alan Ramsay Hawley, president of the Aero Club of America.

Orteig noted that, "As a stimulus to the courageous aviators, I desire to offer, through the auspices and regulations of the Aero Club of America, a prize of $25,000 to the first aviator of any Allied Country crossing the Atlantic in one flight, from Paris to New York or New York to Paris, all other details in your care."

It was a book (first noted by Gregg Maryniak) about that very prize, one ultimately won by Charles Lindbergh via a flight that truly challenged conventional concepts of travel all around the world, that inspired Dr. Peter Diamandis to jump-start a program to inspire a new race to space via a program that would come to be known as the Ansari XPRIZE.

The nascent XPRIZE Foundation authorized the Ansari XPRIZE to engage in a competition for a US $10 million dollar prize for the first non-government entity to launch a reusable manned spacecraft into space… not just once, but TWICE within the space of two weeks. The prize was created in 1996, created a bit of a fury, and then died down a bit while dozens of teams signaled their desire and intention to compete. While raising the prize money was tough, a multi-million dollar donation from entrepreneurs Anousheh Ansari and Amir Ansari eventually made the XPRIZE a real competition with a real 'BIG BUCKS' prize—and some very real players working earnestly to be the first to claim it.

But the XPRIZE program did more than inspire a single competition… it gave rise to a number of innovations, programs and ideas, among them the Zero-Gravity Corporation, Rocket Racing League, Google Lunar XPRIZE, XPRIZE Cup and countless personal and professional adventures that inspired millions around the world.

And God help me… I lived, floated, flew, photographed, documented, and drank it all in as greedily as I could… as the CEO of the Aero-News Network as well as an accomplished photographer and test pilot, there was no place in the XPRIZE world that I ultimately did not get to go… high or low, fast or slow, private or public, safe or risky… and the result is that, along with my trusty Canon SLRs, I got to record some extraordinary history so that I can bring it here to you all now…

Sit down, strap in and hold on (tight!)…

This, folks, was a wild ride. I kid you not…

I mean—wow… just… wow. I have to check now and then for myself… but yes… it really happened. As a matter of fact, it had to be real… I never had dreams that were nearly this wild before, so it must be real… right?

Peter Diamandis, Jim Campbell, and Byron Lichtenberg

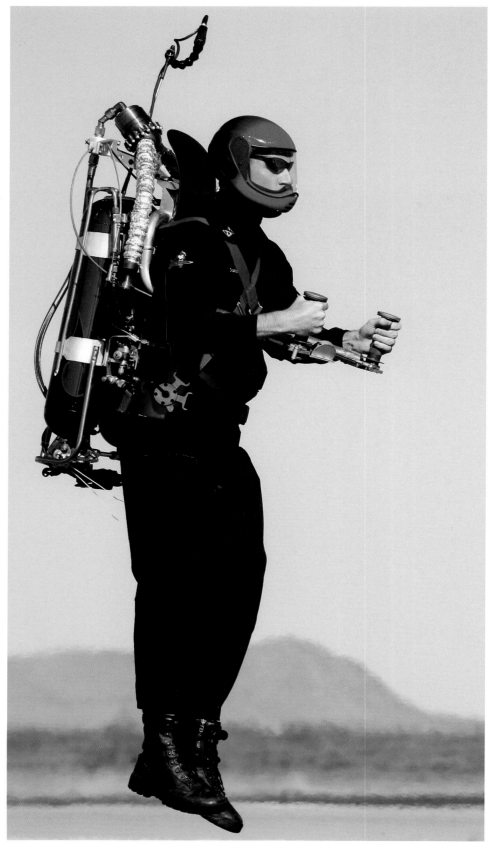

Left: Rocketman Dan Schlund, XPRIZE Cup 2006
Above: 'Pixel'—Armadillo Aerospace, XPRIZE Cup 2006
Right: Burt Rutan and Mike Melvill

Google Lunar XPRIZE Unveiling—Bob Weiss, Larry Page, Peter Diamandis, Buzz Aldrin

"I think the [Ansari] XPRIZE should be viewed as the beginning of one giant leap…"

—Dr. Buzz Aldrin

The Winglet of an Early Prototype Rocket Racer

The Award of the $10M Ansari XPRIZE Check in St. Louis, 2004

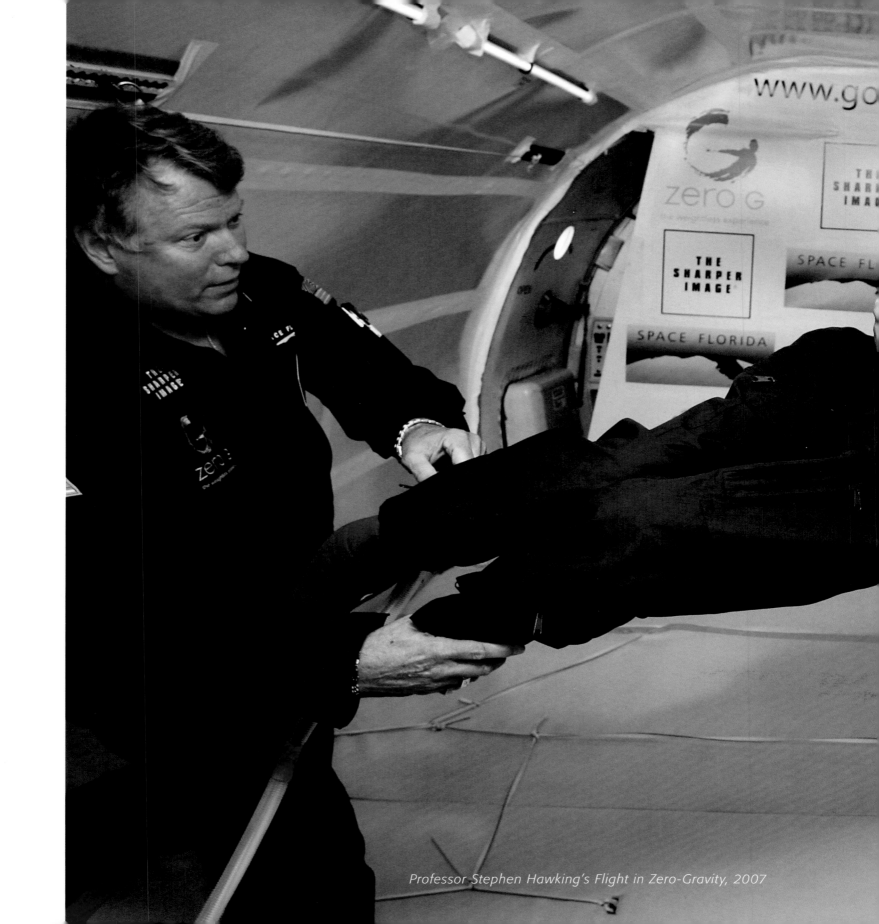

Professor Stephen Hawking's Flight in Zero-Gravity, 2007

Peter Diamandis, XPRIZE, Zero-G

John Carmack, Armadillo Aerospace

The Conjoined Twins

“ Risk is the single biggest thing that we're not doing anymore…
We've become so risk-adverse in society, and that is killing the space
program. Governments and large corporation can't take risks anymore,
for fear of congressional inquiries and lawsuits… But someone has to.”

—Dr. Peter Diamandis

The XPRIZE: Imagine The *Ultimate* Competition—One That Everybody Wins

We are (by nature, if not genetic disposition) a competitive species… as we evolved, we competed with the world around us to stay fed, keep warm, and build the families, groups, efforts, and societies that would eventually allow us to organize and compete with the universe itself for a means to empower our destinies.

It is that sense of competition that has given us a better world, better lives, and a better future to live up to. But to compete, one has to accept the risks of failure and loss…and as societies mature, so does their aversion to anything that may impact the comfort of their lives… no matter how great the benefits.

So… we pioneers take risks—while the non-pioneers look in awe and wonder.

The age-old joke of being able to tell the pioneers from the non-participants by counting the number of arrows in their backsides is often bandied about, but despite those arrows and the ever-present possibility of failure, it is the sweet allure of progress and adventure that drives pioneers forward… with caution, with hope and with courage.

XPRIZE was nothing, if not a pioneering effort, at a time when nations and societies were getting WAY too comfortable with the status quo, and needed wake-up calls like this to again realize what potential the future held. Think about it… America actually got bored with seeing men land and walk on the Moon as soon it was repeated a few times, and ultimately abandoned the pursuit.

"We live in a society that is way too risk adverse, and that is a big problem. The only way we got to the moon in 1969 was by taking risks. Without risks there can't be breakthroughs, and without breakthroughs we stay right where we are."

Indeed.

Amen.

Those are the words of Dr. Peter Diamandis…

A guy who gave up a promising future as a doctor by deciding that his potential effect on the lives of individuals wasn't quite as compelling as the effect he might have on an entire world. Peter gave the world a gift of great and lofty new dreams... the right to think that the wonders of the space-age might be theirs to enjoy. Throughout the events seen in this book, we had unusual access to Peter... traveling with him for a few weeks on board G-Force One while showing the world that the delights of Zero-Gravity are now a civilian pursuit, being selected as one of the founding test pilots for the Rocket Racing League, serving as XPRIZE's news team during the world-changing XPRIZE competition—and so much more.

When you spend that much time with someone, you get to know them well... too well, sometimes. That's when you find whether the person you perceive as a visionary is either an opportunist or the real thing... and Peter, we must tell you, is very much the real thing... a man who looks to the future with great hopes and an eye to crafting it in such a way as to make the seemingly impossible, the next exciting reality.

The world needs a lot more guys like this, and we're pleased that the world has him. And, frankly, we could use a few more.

But even more important than Peter was to this effort, were those who created the organization,

SpaceShipOne and WhiteKnightOne PreFlight Checks, 2004

infrastructure and mechanisms that made XPRIZE possible… most notably guys like Gregg Maryniak—who inspired Peter to the mission that became his life's work during a GA flight in which the Orteig Prize, the inspiration for Charles Lindbergh's transatlantic moment of history was discussed, and eventually assumed as the model for the XPRIZE.

There are so many heroes and extraordinary people in the XPRIZE story… but each of them had a cadre of friends, family, supporters, critics and staff that made their contributions possible.

Take one of the other pivotal people in this tale… Burt Rutan.

We'd be shortchanging everyone at Scaled Composites, Burt Rutan especially, if we put the spotlight, solely, on the side-burned wonder of Mojave. Aviation's Desert Genius established himself as an amazing figurehead—but it was the crew he assembled that made all things possible… and allow his work to be continued, even now, when Burt is somewhat 'retired.' As a former Long-EZ (an experimental aircraft design that pretty much established Burt as an Aero-God) pilot/owner, I can well testify to the abilities of this talented designer (and how cool his birds fly). But more than his skills as an Engineer, it's his sense of vision for the future of aviation and aerospace that impresses us all to blazes. The guy

Starship Chase Pilot, Robert Scherer

simply has a knack for making the most amazing things work… and work well—and (most important, possibly) of building a team that can carry out complex visions that were but science fiction a short time before.

Mind you; every few years, over the course of his career, we heard that Burt had bitten off more than he could chew… but it's people who take such big bites out of life and are willing to attempt what all others say is not possible that makes the aerospace world so fascinating and assures that our future is going to be more interesting than we can imagine.

But… in 2004, Burt, (inspired to even greater imaginings by the allure of the XPRIZE) kicked all the doubting thomases in the butt and proved that ingenuity, imagination and teamwork are even more powerful than NASA's most powerful boosters and collectively capable of bringing man to the threshold of space.

"Since Yuri Gagarin and Al Shepard's epic flights in 1961, all space missions have been flown only under large, expensive Government efforts. By contrast, our program involves a few, dedicated individuals who are focused entirely on making spaceflight afford-

able," said Burt. "Without the entrepreneur approach, space access would continue to be out of reach for ordinary citizens. The SpaceShipOne flights will change all that and encourage others to usher in a new, low-cost era in space travel."

This changes the way an entire world looks at the stars.

And this, above all else, was the mission of XPRIZE … to change the way that the world looked at what was possible (and more than a few things that were thought to be impossible) and to inspire everyone to reach farther than ever before.

And so the first XPRIZE was born… a $10 million prize offer to the first private team to build and launch a spacecraft capable of carrying three people to 100 kilometers above the earth's surface, not once, but twice within two weeks.

The Ansari XPRIZE enticed 26 teams from 7 different nations to pursue their dreams by competing to build a new future. Those 26 teams, all combined, spent more than $100 million to win the prize and spawned an industry that has already created over a billion dollars in economic activity.

The world hasn't been the same since…

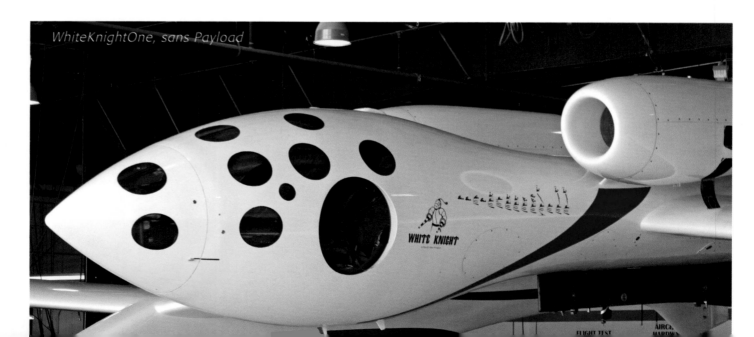
WhiteKnightOne, sans Payload

"My Grandfather was motivated to make his flight by a prize that unquestionably helped to open the future of aviation… I am promoting the XPRIZE because I believe it will help open the door to space travel for the rest of us."

—Erik Lindbergh

Shortly before the Drop, WhiteKnightOne Climbs to Launch Altitude with SpaceShipOne

33

One of Many Close Chats between Burt Rutan and Mike Melvill

06.21.04: The First Sub-Orbital Proving Flight

In the late spring of 2004, the word went out that one team, in particular, was readying an attempt at a flight that would match, and possibly exceed, the tasks required from the Ansari XPRIZE… and it was little or no surprise to many in the aviation and aerospace world that the project was led by maverick aircraft designer Burt Rutan—an iconic and prolific aircraft designer that designed some pivotal airframes… including the globe-girdling Voyager… the first airplane to fly around the world on a single tank of gas… flown by his brother Dick and his partner, Jeana Yeager.

Burt was an unconventional guy… with an unconventional guy's desire for unique, workable solutions to big problems… and he had compiled an enviable track record for succeeding where others either muddled through (barely) or failed completely.

But the big question was… was this amazing contraption… a large gangly mothership and a smaller bullet-shaped pocket rocket that used RUBBER as a propulsion component, REALLY going to loft itself beyond the blue, past the boundaries of our atmosphere and off into REAL LIVE space… to take a place in history?

The Rutan solution, via his Mojave, CA-based Scaled Composites operation was a two-ship program.

According to Burt's people, "To reach space, a carrier aircraft, the White Knight, lifts SpaceShipOne from the runway. An hour later, after climbing to approximately 50,000 feet altitude just east of Mojave, the White Knight releases the spaceship into a glide. The spaceship pilot then fires his rocket motor for about 80 seconds, reaching Mach 3 in a vertical climb. During the pull-up and climb, the pilot encounters G-forces three to four times the gravity of the earth.

SpaceShipOne then coasts up to its goal height of 100 km (62 miles) before falling back to earth. The pilot experiences a weightless environment for more than three minutes and, like orbital space travelers, sees the black sky and the thin blue atmospheric line on the horizon. The pilot (actually a new astronaut!) then configures the craft's wing and tail into a high-drag configuration. This provides a 'care-free' atmospheric entry by slowing the spaceship in the upper atmosphere and automatically aligning it along the flight path. Upon re-entry, the pilot reconfigures the ship back to a normal glider, and then spends 15 to 20 minutes gliding back to earth, touching down like an airplane on the same runway from which he took off. The June flight will be flown solo, but SpaceShipOne is equipped with three seats and is designed for missions that include pilot and two passengers."

When I arrived at Mojave Spaceport in mid-June (the airport had gotten a new designation as a Spaceport by virtue of its designation as a launch point for the Rutan 'Scaled Composites' program), I had extraordinary access to everything I needed to document the birth of a new industry… save one… While working with the XPRIZE and SCALED crews, I was stunned to find out that no plans had been made to put a photographer aboard any of the chase ships that would be shadowing SpaceShipOne on its way to history. A little nonplussed, I put together my gear,

assumed the role of pool photographer for pictures that were shortly to become some of the most published in the world and saddled up aboard Robert Scherer's magnificent Beech Starship… one of the few remaining examples of a Rutan rarity… a successful design program for an unconventional yet magnificent aircraft that got mucked up by the manufacturer and failed to find much of a market.

For the next few hours, the adventure took on breathtaking speed and proportions… as Bob Scherer coaxed the mighty twin-engine turboprop to the brink of 50,000 feet and flew a solid formation in the rarified air above the California desert… nearly high enough there to start detecting the Earth's curvature for ourselves.

The sights, the sounds, the atmosphere of the event took on Science Fiction-like proportions… with most (if not all) involved displaying incredulous grins along with expressive faces that spoke aloud the "Holy (Deleted)—I can't believe we're doing this" feelings shared by one and all.

Just Prior to the First Sub-Orbital Flight, June 21, 2004

"The biggest problem with space flight is neither technical nor regulatory; it is that there is just not enough of it. The number of commercial launches has been low since the mid-1990s; from an economics perspective, there needs to be more. The way for space flight to get cheaper and safer is to do much more of it."

—**Gregg Maryniak, Singularity University, XPRIZE Foundation**

Climbing through 35,000 Feet, over California's Mojave Desert

Mojave International Spaceport

On the Way Up...

On the Way Back Down... Note the Slight Deformation in the Fairing over the Exhaust Bell

Making History.... Mike Melvill Touches Down with Chuck Coleman Keeping a Watchful Eye from His Extra 300

All Alone... WhiteKnightOne is Gangly—Much More So without a Spaceship Attached

A Little Undignified—SpaceShipOne is Towed back to the Hangar

“Mission Summary: Flight 60L / 15P
Date: 21 June 04
Flight Time: 1.6 hour/24 min, 05 sec
White Knight Pilot: Binnie, White Knight Copilot: Stinemetze
SpaceShipOne Pilot: Melvill
High Chase Alpha Jet Crew: Van der Schueren/Johnson
High Chase-Starship Crew: Karkow/Scherer
Low Chase-Extra Crew: Coleman/Bird”

Yet Another Chat between Burt and Mike—This Was a Common Sight That Day

Little Known Fact... SpaceShipOne Has No Nosewheel—Just a Nose-Skid

Scaled Composites Fielded a Large Team of Rocket Professionals Who Inspected SS1 Aggressively Just prior to the First Sub-Orbital Flight

At AirVenture 2005, Mike Melvill and Scott Crossfield (First Pilot to Break Mach Two) compared their rides to space. Mike showered endless praise on Crossfield, calling him "his hero." Crossfield returned just as many good natured humorous jabs at Melvill, at one point replying to the question, 'how did it feel after your first release from the B-52?' "I didn't have time for psycho analysis, I was busy working," said Crossfield. "I was flying an airplane. I don't know what you were doing!"

To which Melvill responded "Well, I was scared!"

" The Meek shall inherit the Earth. The rest of us will go to the Stars"

—As seen on the back of a shirt worn by a teenage girl

Final Inspections before Flight

X1: OK... One For The Money....

With the success of the June 21st flight safely in the rear-view mirror and all issues pretty much put to rest, the American Mojave Aerospace Ventures, LLC Team (the actual partnership between Paul G. Allen and Burt Rutan and his team at Scaled Composites) gave the required 60-day notice and scheduled its first competition flight on September 29th, 2004, at the Mojave Airport Civilian Aerospace Test Center in Mojave, California. To win the $10 million, SpaceShipOne needed to make a second flight within two weeks (by October 13th, 2004). The second flight was tentatively scheduled for October 4th, 2004, the 47th Anniversary of the Sputnik launch.

The historic flight revolved around two unique vehicles… the only iterations of their kind. Scaled Composites described SpaceShipOne as a three-place, high-altitude research rocket, designed for sub-orbital flights to 100 km altitude. The unique configuration allows aircraft-like qualities for boost, glide, and landing. The ship converts (via pneumatic-actuated feather) to a stable, high-drag shape for atmospheric entry. This 'care-free' configuration allows a 'hands-off' re-entry and greatly reduces aero/thermal loads. Designed for a 'shirt-sleeve' environment, the 60" diameter cabin has a space-qualified ECS, as well as dual-pane windows. The ship uses three flight control systems—manual-subsonic, electric-supersonic and cold-gas RCS. SpaceShipOne's hybrid rocket motor is a non-toxic, liquid nitrous-oxide/rubber-fuel hybrid propulsion system. The avionics onboard provide the pilot with the precise guidance information needed to manually fly SpaceShipOne for boost and re-entry. It also provides guidance for approach and landing and vehicle health monitoring. The unit stores and telemeters flight test data to mission control.

The White Knight was described as a manned, twin-turbojet research aircraft intended for high-altitude missions. The first flight was on August 1, 2002, and it's design mission provides a high-altitude airborne launch of SpaceShipOne, a manned sub-orbital spacecraft. The White Knight is equipped to flight-qualify all the spacecraft systems, except rocket propulsion. The White Knight's cockpit, avionics, ECS, pneumatics, trim servos, data system, and electrical system components are identical to those installed on SpaceShipOne. The White Knight's high thrust-to-weight ratio and enormous speed brakes allow the astronauts in training to practice space flight maneuvers such as boost, approach, and landing with a very realistic environment. Thus, the aircraft serves as a high-fidelity moving-base simulator for SpaceShipOne pilot training.

Like the June 21st proving flight, this flight was piloted by Mike Melvill. The flight was scientific in purpose but very personal in nature. Burt Rutan revealed that the ashes of his mother were flown aboard the spacecraft on this flight—while Melvill said it was an honor to carry her remains. Mike, himself, carried his wife Sally's wedding ring—which had only left her finger one other time in 43 years of marriage.

After some weather concerns, mostly over winds, the White Knight/SpaceShipOne combined vehicle lifted off to join the chase ships, including the Beech Starship from which I monitored the flight and shot the photos that documented this effort.

The flight was dramatic... After separation and ignition into the boost phase of the flight (where it left White Knight and those of us in the chase-ships like the proverbial bat out of hell); SpaceShipOne began an unexpected right roll, turning over and over until well after Melvill initiated the engine cut. Despite that anomaly, Melvill was able to break the 62 mile minimum, meeting the first XPrize requirement

with an altitude of 337,600 feet. Using the Reaction Control System, Mike regained proper control of the spacecraft's attitude and on the long glide back from space, was heard over the radio joking with other crew members about his harrowing experience. A control check, along with close visual inspections by the chase planes, indicated there is no structural damage resulting from the unexpected roll.

"I was kind of worried about that," said Burt's brother, Dick Rutan, who was providing commentary for coverage of the event—referring to the rapid series of rolls. But he said that if anyone could handle such an in-flight anomaly, it would have to be Melvill.

"When that kind of thing happens, Mike slows down and deals with it."

The resultant, and thankfully anti-climactic, landing was a good one... the anticipation intense... the flight had some issues... issues that would need to be resolved... and a two week window in which to do it all again to take the Ansari XPRIZE and the $10 million that goes with it.

September 29th, 2004—X1!

With a Lot of New Decals Adorning Both Mothership and Spaceship, X1 Got Off to a Brilliant Start

But… Rutan was confident in their plan… Studies of what occurred were quickly analyzed and transmitted by Rutan, "While the first roll occurred at a high true speed, about 2.7 Mach, the aerodynamic loads were quite low (120 KEAS) and were decreasing rapidly, so the ship never saw any significant structural stresses. The reason that there were so many rolls was because shortly after they started, Mike was approaching the extremities of the atmosphere. Nearly all of the 29 rolls that followed the initial departure were basically at near-Zero-G, thus they were a continuous rolling motion without aerodynamic damping, rather than the airplane-like aerodynamic rolls seen by an aerobatic airplane. In other words, they were more like space flight than they were like airplane flight. Thus, Mike could not damp the motions with his aerodynamic flight controls.

Mike elected to wait until he feathered the boom-tail in space, before using the reaction control system thrusters (RCS) to damp the roll rate. When he finally started to damp the rates he did so successfully and promptly. The RCS damping, to a stable attitude without significant angular rates was complete well before the ship reached apogee (337,600 feet, or 103 Km). That gave Mike time to relax, note his peak altitude, and then pick up a digital high-resolution camera and take some great photos out the windows…

While we did not plan the rolls, we did get valuable engineering data on how well our RCS system works in space to damp high angular rates. We also got a further evaluation of our 'Care-free Reentry' capability, under a challenging test condition. As seen on the videos of the flight, the ship righted itself quickly and accurately without pilot input as it fell straight into the atmosphere. No other winged, horizontal-landing spaceship (X-15, Buran, Space Shuttle) has this capability."

In a short period of time, Rutan would confirm that his team would need far less than the maximum two weeks to prep and launch SpaceShipOne for the final task necessary to win the XPRIZE. In less than a week, October 4th, SpaceShipOne would fly again—and history would be made.

Re-Joining over Mojave at Close to 40,000 Feet

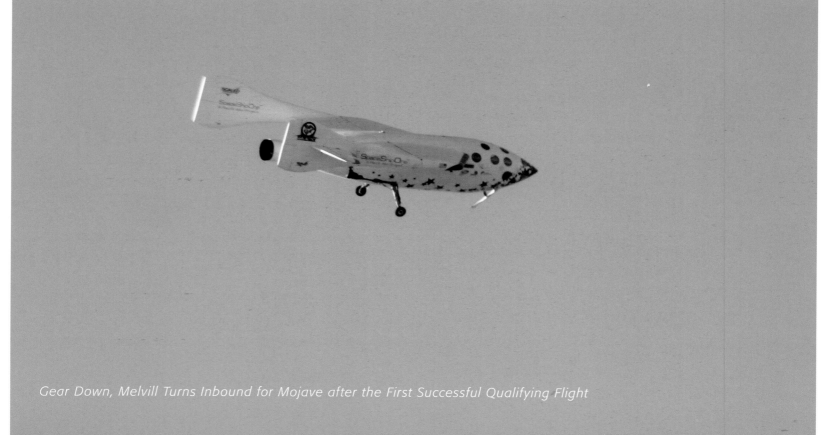

Gear Down, Melvill Turns Inbound for Mojave after the First Successful Qualifying Flight

Turning in for Final Approach

Chuck Coleman and His Extra 300 Inspects SS1 as It Prepares for Touchdown

One of the Many Chase Aircraft that Supported the Test and Qualifying Flights—
Bob Scherer's Hard-Working Beech Starship (A Rutan Design)

Post Flight Press Conference: Burt Rutan, Mike Melvill, Peter Diamandis

Mike Melvill   Peter Diamandis

X2: Making History The Hard Way

Halfway to history… that's how it felt… and indeed, that was what was in the offing… the midpoint in the first major test of the XPRIZE revolution. Barely able to catch one's breath from the first qualifying flight just a few days before, the XPRIZE team and Burt's crews were in a fever pitch to make sure that the second flight, and the final task on the way to winning the Ansari competition, was not only successful but a true vindication of all they had worked for.

And it was all that… in well under the 14 days required to repeat the lofty goals of the first flight, it was Brian Binnie that was ultimately selected to take SpaceShipOne through the final hurdle and into the history books.

Mike Melvill, who had flown two successful test flights in SS1, including the first qualifying XPRIZE flight, was questioned incessantly about whether or not he was going to get to fly the final XPRIZE flight… At the time, the ID of the pilot was a closely guarded secret (though my ANN organization had found about the ID earlier and held on to the details per Rutan's request).

Mike responded to the queries, "The last leg? No one has announced who's gonna fly it. I'd love to see someone else get the chance at it. I'm feeling greedy right now, it seems like I grab all the flights, and

I'd love to see someone else get a chance. The other guys have practiced just as hard as I have, they've worked just as hard. They're younger, they have faster reflexes, and they're better in many ways than I am. And I'd love to see one of them get a shot at it. But of course, if no one else wants the flight, I'd be happy to do it."

Binnie's flight went well and earned an instant spot in the history books… but some of the behind-the-scenes details are amusing…

While he was wishing 'cheerio' to family and friends before Monday's SpaceShipOne flight, pilot Brian Bennie inadvertently took on 12 ounces more weight than planned.

"My mother-in-law was there with a cup of coffee, she put her arms around me, wished me well, and this coffee went down the back of my neck… So we were about 12 ounces heavier than planned."

Referring to the experience itself, Binnie recalled the first flight in which Mike Melvill rolled 29 times.

"Burt (Rutan) tends to couch everything in terms of fun," he said. "After Mike's flight, Burt said, 'Okay, that's enough fun.' It wasn't as much 'fun' as Mike's, but we went a little bit higher, and it was a joy."

He called the initial feeling at ignition 'a rush' and

that the world wakes up around you. It was similar to the descriptions given by Melvill during his presentations at EAA AirVenture 2004. "You get into the arena with the bull, open the gate, and off you go," Binnie said.

Binnie took some quick pictures that he called spectacular, but nothing to compare to the view to the human eye. "It is a thrill that everybody should have once in a lifetime and I am certainly privileged to have seen it this morning."

Binnie was asked that since Melvill let go of some M&Ms when he went up the first time in June, so did he release anything? "At the last minute I was not going to try and do any one-upmanship of Mike with a competing brand like Skittles," he said. "But somebody did hand me a paper model of SpaceShipOne, and I got it out and as I was up there free-falling, a little model of SpaceShipOne was free-falling within SpaceShipOne, so that was cool for me."

The final flight, 'X2,' was nearly as perfect as imaginable, with no rolls such as those that had occurred during Melvill's X1 flight. Binnie credited the team at Scaled Composites with working tirelessly to solve the anomaly.

"We got up there with no rates at all, essentially. I actually used RCS (reaction control system thrusters) just to get a different orientation out the window so I could get a different picture."

To those on the ground, history came on a bright sunny desert day… In a scene reminiscent of Edwards AFB during the days of Yeager and Crossfield. The formation of SpaceShipOne and the chase airplanes circle overhead and then escorts SpaceShipOne onto final. Astronaut Pilot Binnie drops the landing gear and greases his spacecraft onto the runway centerline as the throng of spectators roar in approval.

History.

After SpaceShipOne comes to a halt and the ground support vehicles race to its side, White Knight and the other support aircraft make a graceful low pass over the scene. Minutes later SpaceShipOne is towed to the ramp area near the VIP fence where Binnie, his arms holding out an American flag, stands atop it in a celebration of the day's event as well as the future to which it will lead.

Behind the fence everyone has a sense of the implications that this flight goes far beyond the XPRIZE. The excitement extends out into the future of space travel and the very real possibility that you too may be able to one day fly in space.

The event itself went smoothly and swiftly… and it seemed over and done all too soon… leaving an exhausted XPRIZE community to absorb the import of the victory and the chance to start dreaming about what may occur next.

Those dreams and ideas flowed freely throughout the days that followed… interrupted only by the chance to gather once again in St. Louis to celebrate the winning of what many thought highly improbable, if not impossible, just a few years before.

The XPRIZE had made history… and it wasn't even remotely done yet.

On October 4, 2004, SpaceShipOne became the first private manned spacecraft to exceed an altitude of 328,000 feet twice within two weeks (barely one, actually) and claimed the $10 million dollar prize.

There was some other interesting history mixed in all this… in addition to pushing past the 100KM border, pilot Brian Binnie also blitzed past the August 22, 1963 record of Joseph A. Walker, who flew the X-15 to an unofficial world altitude record of 354,200 feet. Binnie's flight lofted him all the way to 367,442 feet—some 69.6 miles above the Earth's surface. Above and beyond all that, the October 4, 2004 SpaceShipOne final XPRIZE task coincided with the 47th anniversary of the Soviet launch of Sputnik.

History… on top of history… on top of history.

“You get into the arena with the bull, open the gate, and off you go.”

—SpaceShipOne Pilot, Brian Binnie

Tears of Joy... Anousheh Ansari Sees Her Dream Coming to Life

The FAA's Patti Grace Smith, FAA Administrator Blakey, Harry Diamandis and His Son, Peter

> "The XPRIZE will put us back on track in fulfilling our natural quest for human exploration."

—Tom Clancy, Author

"This flight is one of the most exciting and challenging activities taking place in the fields of aviation and aerospace today. Every time SpaceShipOne flies we demonstrate that relatively modest amounts of private funding can significantly increase the boundaries of commercial space technology. Burt Rutan and his team at Scaled Composites have accomplished amazing things by conducting the first mission of this kind without any government backing."

—Paul G. Allen, Sole Sponsor of the SpaceShipOne program

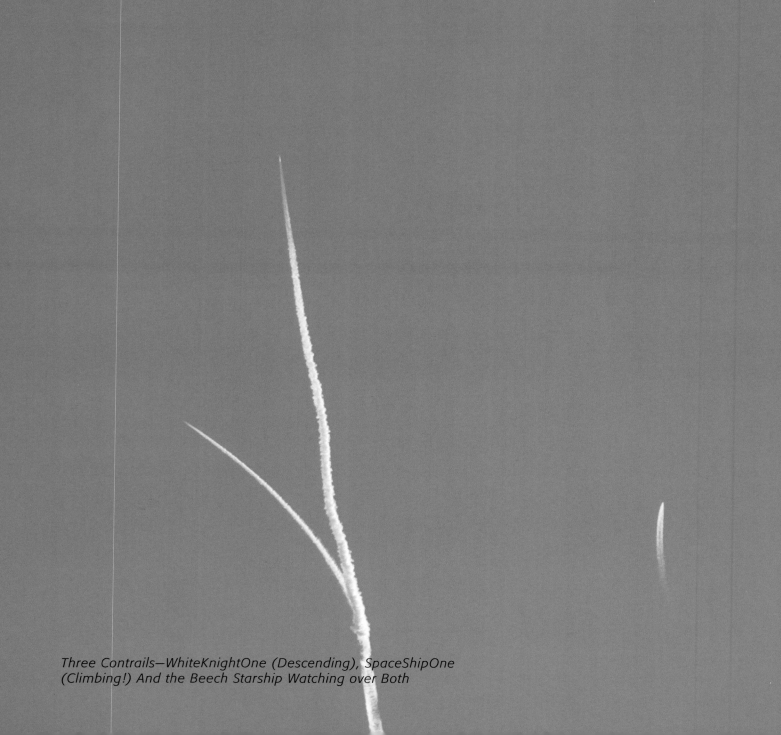

Three Contrails—WhiteKnightOne (Descending), SpaceShipOne (Climbing!) And the Beech Starship Watching over Both

Coming Home: Chuck Coleman's Extra 300, SpaceShipOne and the Alpha Jet

Touchdown! Brian Binnie's Triumphant Flight Returns to Earth

Paul Allen, Burt Rutan, Brian Binnie and Peter Diamandis Celebrate

"My mother-in-law was there with a cup of coffee, she put her arms around me, wished me well, and this coffee went down the back of my neck. So we were about 12 ounces heavier than planned."

—SpaceShipOne Pilot, Brian Binnie

Celebration!!!

Brian Binnie Waves the Flag

ANSARI

X

WORLD SERIES

XPRIZE St. Louis:
Celebrating *THE* New Frontier

St. Louis Celebrates Another Major Aero-Victory

In the shadow of the great city of St. Louis, on the grounds of the St. Louis Science Center, forward thinking members of the local community as well as the rest of the XPRIZE team, gathered together to celebrate the 'loss' of $10 million dollars and the award of the Ansari XPRIZE $10M check and trophy.

History was made when an enterprising team of aerospace professionals took on the challenge posed by Dr. Peter Diamandis eight years before... to build the first steps on man's road to making space travel available to the common man.

SpaceShipOne and Mojave Aerospace Ventures, LLC, reached for the stars and nearly 370,000 feet later, they had won the $10 million Ansari XPRIZE. Pilot Brian Binnie soared WAY past the threshold of space (328,000'), also breaking the August 22, 1963 record set by Joseph A. Walker who flew the X-15 to an unofficial world altitude record of 354,200 feet.

In a number of public and private events over the course of two days, Rutan, his team, Paul Allen, Erik Lindbergh, and the entire XPRIZE and New Spirit of St. Louis teams gathered together and celebrated in a way that has probably not been seen since 1927.

Interestingly, many noted that the XPRIZE achievement seems to have been subject to the 'Rule of the 8's.' It took eight years for the challenge of the Orteig prize to be realized in Charles Lindbergh's magnificent flight across the Atlantic... it took eight years for John Kennedy's 1961 challenge to be realized in man's first steps on the surface of the moon and it took eight years for Rutan's team to meet the challenge posed in 1996 by XPRIZE Founder Peter Diamandis... but it was a helluva eight years.

There were a number of unique moments to be had over that weekend's superb events...

The attendance of many of the Scaled Composites team—who were ferried to St. Louis in Paul Allen's private 757...

Bob Scherer's well-timed fly-over in the Beech Starship Chase-Plane—just as the morning awards were concluding...

NASA's Bill Readdy acknowledging his debt to model rocketry and the dreams inspired by Science Fiction writer Robert Heinlein before raising his glass in salute to the victorious team that launched SpaceShipOne...

The video of Burt Rutan's speech to the inaugural XPRIZE dinner EIGHT years before...

And the overall sense of giddy certainty that came every time hands were raised, en masse, to answer the question—"How many of you want to go to space?"

Rutan was to be busy as soon as he returned to Mojave. The majority of the design work needed to make SpaceShipTwo a reality, awaited—the victorious team having been contracted by Sir Richard Branson to commence work on Virgin Galactic, a sub-orbital tourism program based on a commercial derivative of SpaceShipOne.

Flights are expected to cost about US$200,000 per person (and expected to get less expensive as the program matures). The new spaceship will be able to accommodate one pilot and five passengers.

"We're very proud that the Ansari XPRIZE Competition has helped to spawn this new industry," said Peter H. Diamandis, Chairman of the XPRIZE. "This is exactly the results we hoped this $10M purse would create."

Overall, the award ceremonies made for an amazing weekend—and it is but one of many to come... because the award of the XPRIZE is not about the end of a dream, but the full realization of the altogether new, incredible, future that the dream has inspired—as was repeated throughout the weekend, over and over again...

"Take our word for it... You ain't seen nothing yet."

Signing Autographs—Much of the XPRIZE Team Received a Lot of Practice at This

Some of the Many Happy Faces of the XPRIZE Celebration (clockwise): Eric Lindbergh, Peter Diamandis, Burt Rutan

The Ansari XPRIZE Trophy

Erik Lindbergh

The Payoff... Nearly Decades after the Dream, It was Time to Pay Up!

On the check:

0001

DATE *November 06, 2004*

Inc. $ **10,000,000.00**

and 00/100   DOLLARS

H. DIAMANDIS
n & Founder

ROBERT K. WEISS
Vice Chairman

GREGG MARYNIAK
Executive Director

00

The Diamandis Family: Dr. Peter H. Diamandis, His Wife Kristen, His Sister Marcelle, His Mother Tula and His Father, Dr. Harry P. Diamandis

Zero-G: 'The Floaty Dream'

Let's Talk Zero-G!

Zero-Gravity... is amazing.

And while many people may never be able to afford the $200,000 dollars necessary to buy a seat on SpaceShipTwo, a few thousand dollars will get you several minutes of delicious Zero-G, thirty extraordinary seconds at a time. I got to help Peter Diamandis and our other partners start the first commercial Zero-G airline... which has grown to not only conduct hundreds of safe commercial flights up to this point... but has proven to be so dependable and well-managed that it now conducts these same services for NASA... and get this... it makes money.

The Zero-G concept was yet another dream of a number of people... to take the technology and procedures already well-proven in NASA operations, and allow real-live everyday people to play in Zero-G to their hearts content. For nearly 50 years, NASA had plied the skies of the world with a modified KC-135, somewhat derisively known as the 'Vomit Comet,' doing Zero-G research and training future aerospace professionals. Only a very few got the coveted chance to experience the extraordinary effects of NO GRAVITY as NASA's exclusive group of flyers was a pretty small club. You either had to be an astronaut, a scientist or a lucky journalist to get on board—and even then, competition for slots on those flights was known to be pretty tough.

That was then.... this is now.

In 2004, an 11-year dream OFFICIALLY came to fruition as the nascent (then) Zero-G Corporation inaugurated FAA certified FAR Part 121 flights. These adventures featured numerous demonstrations of parabolic flight, inducing temporarily lessened gravitational effects and allowing a few dozen fliers, at a time, to feel what it's like to walk on Mars (approximately 1/3G), the Moon (about 1/6G) and even the weightlessness of space (the world's greatest weight loss plan... NO WEIGHT AT ALL!).

The procedure was well-known... but had never been subjected to the rigors of FAA certification. Both I and a number of my compatriots at Aero-News were privileged to enjoy Zero-G quite a number of times and I was a part of the original team that saw the process through to certification.

Once the FAA got through throwing obstacles and barriers in the way of progress (rumor has it that the FAA is not satisfied with any certification process until the weight of the resulting paper work exceeds the gross weight of the aircraft involved... and this appears to have been the case with Zero-G, as well.

When everything was finally accepted and certified, the process was a fairly simple one. Aboard a lightly modified Boeing 727 that went by the name of 'G-FORCE ONE' (a far more palatable name than 'Vomit Comet'), fractions of weightlessness or absolute weightlessness was undertaken via a simple maneuver known as a parabola. A parabola is a very simple thing... but a well-executed parabola, in which a somewhat linear progression from 1G to 1.8Gs and a slow 'push-over' to Zero-G and the resultant recovery from a slight dive at the end of the parabola, is a bit of an art form. Not difficult to learn, a smooth well-executed parabola became a thing of great beauty and produced a lovely transition that resulted in a very nice ride... and over time, a LOT of happy weightless flyers. As the veteran of several thousand parabolas, I was immediately impressed with how well the pilots undertook their chores to not only produce a textbook maneuver (which is, technically, an aerobatic maneuver as the aircraft pitches up to, and occasionally a bit over, 45 degrees pitch negative and positive), but a smooth and fluid sequence that offered maximum comfort to the earliest Zero-G flyers... who really were not sure that they were going to have all that great a time... and with very few exceptions, that's exactly what they had... an adventure of a lifetime.

Today, Zero-G has made this formula work, over and over again... for thousands of people who want to get a dose of what astronauts have such difficulty explaining... an experience that really must be experienced to be able to understand it. As a test pilot and aerobatic pilot whose life has oft revolved around some pretty aggressive 'G' transitions and some pretty radical force gradients, to boot (a few select birds I've flown could offer solid 12 positive and negative-G maneuvering capability), I was often in awe of the precision th4ese pilots developed in wrestling that Boeing through what became, literally, a delicate aerial ballet in their defiance of gravity.

The standard procedure has changed little since we watched the process achieve certification in 2004 (and frankly, it hasn't needed to).

In locations all over the world, today's Zero-G Boeing 727s climbs to approximately 24,000 feet and levels off.

From there, a gradual, linear pitch positive 'pull' on the control yoke produces a solid 45 degrees pitch 'up' attitude and less than 2Gs at the pinnacle of the climb force gradient. Near the top of the 'zoom,' the bird starts a gentle pitch-over (pushing forward in, again, a gradual and linear fashion) some 10,000 higher than where it starts... which results in a pitch-push-over that is undertaken, a few degrees per second, with the negative pitch inclination resulting in the 'cancellation' of gravity (applying a negative force gradient to the positive force/G of gravity) to the extent required by the mission for that parabola... i.e., for each of the three types of parabolas that are designed to produce either 1/3, 1/6 and Zero-Gravity.

The carefully executed weightless segment can allow for 20-30 seconds (or even a few seconds more in the hands of the more-experienced pilots) of reduced or Zero-Gravity... and within the confines of the padded cabin/weightless play area, the dozens of flyers and their coaches are having the time of their lives... in no uncertain terms.

As the maneuver reaches its conclusion, the pilots start a gentle pitch positive 'Pull' on the control yoke, as the now 45 degree descent is required to level out, stabilize the aircraft and prepare to start the sequence, over and over again... a dozen or more time in a flight for the commercial program... and as many as dozens of times for some of the NASA missions. The whole sequence requires about 10-15 miles of airspace (and a maneuver zone of some 100 miles) and 10,000-12,000 feet of airspace each time… part of an area blocked out with the cooperation of ATC to avoid conflicts with other air traffic (though airliners spying such maneuvers from a safe distance have apparently been REALLY amused at watching a Boeing climbing and diving in a very 'Un-Boeing-like' manner.

I've watched hundreds of people come aboard G-Force One with a nervous grin and leave the bird a little over an hour or two later absolutely exhilarated, chattering up a storm… and often wondering about when they might be able to do it again… It's THAT addictive.

There is another side effect… one that can last for years (and, indeed, I still experience them on a regular basis). I (and others) call it, 'The Floaty Dream.' The experience is so profound, influential and personal, that it shows up in one's dreams… again and again… and with the sights, sounds and adrenaline rush, comes that feeling of detachment from gravity… often awaking in such a way as to have to reach out to find something to hold on to… lest one floats away from the bed. And outside of having had to explain one early such iteration to my wife, it is a pleasant and somewhat intimate way to indulge in a memory that can often be life-changing, and most certainly, inspiring.

'The Floaty Dream'—all by itself—is worth the price of taking a ride with Zero-G…

One of the Early Zero-G Crew Compliments

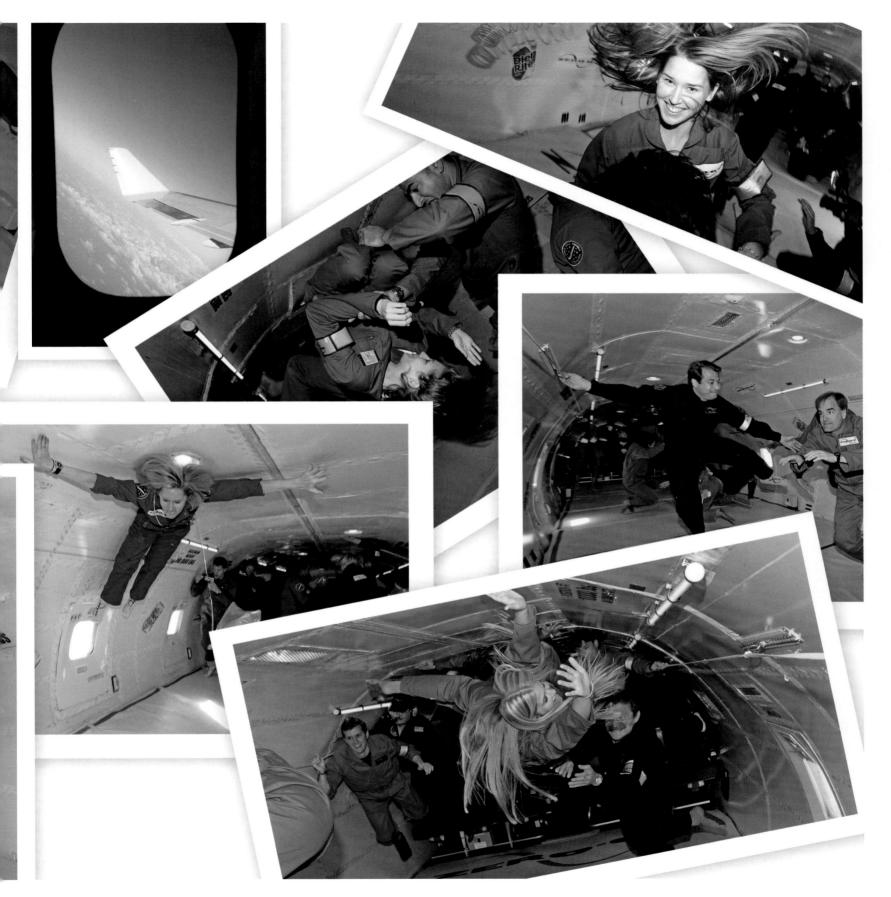

G-Force One is a Mostly Unmodified Boeing 727... An Aircraft That Served ZG Exceptionally Well

Zero-G: Barnstorming The Nation

In the fall of 2004, an ingenious plan to promote and publicize the advent of FAA certified commercial weightless flights was initiated that put 'G-Force One' and a hearty group of Zero-G staff and associates on the road, uh runways, for a few weeks in order to introduce the media, as well as a number of notable persons, to experience the technologies and joys allowed by weightless flight.

Those weeks became some of the most memorable of my life... as much for what I got to do, as for documenting and photographing the people I witnessed as they had their mental, emotional and physical horizons broadened to the extreme.

I saw more joy, more wonder, and more inspirational moments in that period of time than nearly any year(s) in my memory.

It didn't matter who they were... media, dignitaries, business leaders, engineers, test pilots, you name it. It blew them all away.

The only folks who seemed to lack the extreme sense of wonder were those already well acquainted... like a man who had gone to the moon a few decades before... but despite all that, EVERY single one of our weightless wonders had a ball... they all reflected the joy that weightlessness brings, and even the

astronauts and test pilots who had a fair amount of Zero-G time under their belts, showed that despite their familiarity, that weightlessness was an old and valued friend... to be enjoyed, cherished and shared... and they did.

And so it was that Zero-G embarked on a 2 week nationwide tour, in collaboration with its promotion partner, Diet Rite soft drinks. Aero-News and I went along for the ride, as a newsperson, aero-historian, Zero-G's official photographer and a Zero-G coach, to boot... whereupon it became Job One for yours truly to show the terrestrial world what an out-of-this world experience it really was... and to send the principal message—that YOU can do this for yourself.

The sky was no longer the limit...

The Zero-G Barnstorming tour went from coast to coast, it made lots of news, and by the time that it was over, there was a perceptible change in the public perception of private and commercial space endeavors... and all this just a few weeks before the heady victory of the winning of the XPRIZE, which brought the world to the inescapable conclusion that personal space flight was going to be a reality in their lifetimes—and a potentially major part of the lives of their kids.

As a qualified Zero-G coach and photographer, as well as a crew member for this project, most of what I saw then, as well as over the next few years, were delighted, even joyous, faces filled with the wonder of the Zero-Gravity experience. Yes, a few people do not adjust well to the 1.8G to 0G excursions, and some do get sick.

Then again, some people also get carsick.

Some get seasick.

Some people have problems with the most gentle of airline flights... that's life... but that's also the exception, and NOT the rule.

The GREAT majority of Zero-G participants feel nothing but exhilaration... and I've got over 10,000 high resolution photographs to prove it. More important than that, I have worked and trained with the Zero-G company since BEFORE they were FAA certified... I watched them sweat the most minute of details, work through the night to deal with every foreseeable issue, and act with the utmost in professionalism.

I have nothing but the highest respect and admiration for the way that they have conducted themselves (as well as the Amerijet operation that operated the initial aircraft—TOP Notch folks, all) and was pleased to join them on a regular basis for years—including one flight that was set up as a surprise fortieth birthday party for the guest of honor—everyone had a ball, no one got sick, we hit a few bumps and we giggled the entire time.

The world, and its perceptions, changed.

Zero-G had arrived.

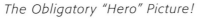
The Obligatory "Hero" Picture!

Former Space Shuttle Commander and Zero-G Coach, Rick Searfoss

I Can't Recall Any Photo I've Taken in Zero-G in Which Everyone Wasn't Smiling

Buzz Aldrin Returns To Familiar Territory: Lunar Gravity

Sharing Some Lunar Gravity Moments With Apollo 11 Astronaut Buzz Aldrin

Just a few days into the inaugural tour of Zero-G Corporation's Boeing 727 weightless inducing wonderplane, an old friend to reduced gravity came on board to sample it for himself... yet again.

Apollo 11 Moonwalker Buzz Aldrin joined XPrize Founder Peter Diamandis, yours truly (who was having a heckuva time, flying and shooting and shooting and flying), and a few dozen other spaceboosters for flights in the modified G-Force One Boeing 727 on promotional flights out of Burbank, CA. This assemblage swiftly headed out over the Pacific and twisted the laws of gravity to suit their lofty purposes with a series of 10 parabolas... and not just once, but twice, that day.

"G-Force One" flew two missions, offering a series of Martian (1/3G), Lunar (1/6G) and Zero-Gravity excursions that thrilled both the newbies on board, as well as the experienced spacefarer.

It was evident to one and all that Dr. Aldrin was prepared to have a ball and was not to be disappointed... Buzz was very gracious, posing for pictures, answering questions and speaking forcefully and positively of the future of private space travel... but when he got turned loose in reduced, as well as zero-gravity, it was obvious that he felt right at home.

More important, he was having a great time.

Aldrin demonstrated a series of somersaults, rolling maneuvers, and an excellent command of zero-gravity maneuvering despite his admission that this was his first chance to work in reduced gravity since the return from the moon. "...outside of some turbulence on airline flights, this is the first time (for reduced gravity) since Apollo," he admitted... with a smile.

Aldrin's accomplishments are impressive— and not just for his flight to the moon. The NASA record shows that on November 11, 1966, Aldrin

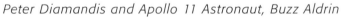
Peter Diamandis and Apollo 11 Astronaut, Buzz Aldrin

Buzz... Inverted

and command pilot James Lovell were launched into space in the Gemini 12 spacecraft on a 4-day flight, which brought the Gemini program to a successful close. Aldrin established a new record for extravehicular activity (EVA), spending 5-1/2 hours outside the spacecraft.

He served as lunar module pilot for Apollo 11, July 16-24, 1969, the first manned lunar landing mission. Aldrin followed Neil Armstrong onto the lunar surface on July 20, 1969, completing a 2-hour and 15 minute lunar EVA.

In July of 1971, Aldrin resigned from NASA, having logged 289 hours and 53 minutes in space, of which, 7 hours and 52 minutes were spent in EVA.

It had been thirty five years since Buzz Aldrin and Neil Armstrong set foot on the moon, on July 20th, 1969; leaving that lonely orb the next day and rocketing home to a permanent place in the record books. In the meantime, he's become a passionate

spokesman for space exploration, a successful businessman, an author, and a particularly persuasive advocate for making the commitments necessary to make space accessible to more people than ever.

More than just a space spokesman, he's a willing participant in this pioneering movement. For a few hours on a Wednesday in 2004, in the midst of Zero-G's great barnstorming adventure, Buzz took his place among a group of regular folks (all in a little awe of the man), showed them a few Zero-G moves, and participated in the first major commercial program designed to offer public access to space-like technology aboard the world's first FAA certified Zero-G airline.

Judging by the many smiles among those on board that day (and many more since), it would seem that Aldrin's arguments to allow private access to space will continue to get wide support from America's first private Zero-G flyers.

One Happy, History-Making Zero-G Flight

Buzz 'Buzzes' the Cameraman

Burt and Boscoe's Excellent Adventure

It was but weeks before a quiet aerospace engineer and his devoted crew of rocket pioneers were to make history and change the world.

I'd been having a ball sharing Zero-G with a number of luminaries aboard 'G-Force One' during an inaugural press tour, but... with the exception of Apollo 11's Buzz Aldrin, none of these VIPs have been as eagerly awaited as Scaled Composites' Burt Rutan.

Aviation Pioneer and SpaceShip One Designer Burt Rutan boarded G-Force One at Mercury Air Center in Burbank, CA, on a September morning in 2004 to experience his first weightless flight.

Accompanying Burt was Scaled's furry mascot, 'Boscoe,' a stuffed bear that was listed to be on the next flight of SpaceShipOne... if he made the grade.

"I brought Boscoe here to see how he handles Zero-G. If he gets sick, he's off the flight," said Burt (totally deadpan, if tongue-in-cheek). Boscoe did well—even ditching Burt for a while to fly around the cabin on his own, visiting with a number of other Zero-G flyers—especially the cute ones.

Burt's own experience was exhilarating—and his handling of Zero-G looked as expert as any of the "old-timers" who have done this many times before.

Burt Rutan Autographs G-Force One... One of the Few Asked to Do So

"'The Zero-G Experience' was ten times better than I expected," noted Burt.

"I highly recommend it for those who want to experience a suborbital flight. It was really amazing, unbelievably cool!"

Rutan experienced one Martian, followed by one Lunar and then 27 Zero-G parabolas. Rutan was, at that time, the leading contender for the XPRIZE competition for which his SpaceShipOne had already flown to a height of 100 kilometers on June 21st in the qualifying flight…and then, just a few weeks later, performed two amazing flights to take the $10 million dollar Ansari XPRIZE and ensure his place in history.

Peter Diamandis, then the founder, chairman, and CEO of the Zero Gravity Corporation said, "I am very proud to be able to have taken Rutan on his first trip to weightlessness. Now he is ready for his suborbital flight."

Boscoe was not available for comment—but his grin never wavered throughout the flight…

Burt Rutan Readies "Boscoe" for the Zero-G Experience

XPRIZE's Gregg Maryniak and SpaceShipOne Designer, Burt Rutan, are Having NO Fun...

"How I wished everyone could experience this feeling in their heart, especially those who are at the head of the governments in the world. Maybe this experience would give them a new perspective and help bring peace to the world."

—Anousheh Ansari

No Matter How Tight the Schedule, There was Always Time for the Obligatory "Hero" Pic!

Awaiting takeoff aboard G-Force One in 2004, Dr. Aldrin admitted that this was his first chance to work in reduced gravity since his return from the moon. "...outside of some turbulence on airline flights, this is the first time (for reduced gravity) since Apollo," he admitted... with a smile.

Peter Gets A Little Time (And Gravity) Off

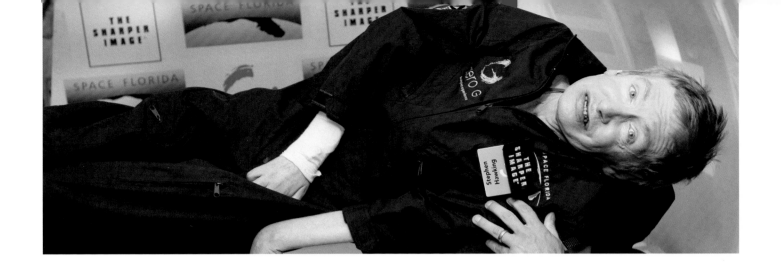

Dreamlike: Flying With Professor Stephen Hawking

A Brief History of a Day in the Life of an 'Amazing' Man

It was a peculiar, albeit brilliant idea. After Zero-G has accomplished the arduous task of introducing weightless flight to thousands of people, they were tasked with the most intriguing flight, to date. Professor Stephen Hawking, a man who studied the makeup of the universe in excruciating, fine detail, wanted to experience Zero-G for himself… hopefully as a prelude to his own flight into space at some unnamed time in the future.

But flying Professor Hawking had some special challenges… Almost completely paralyzed by amyotrophic lateral sclerosis, or Lou Gehrig's disease, his flight would allow him to, temporarily, abandon his wheelchair to try on the aura of weightlessness for himself. Zero-Gravity founder Peter Diamandis took up Hawking's request with a vengeance, knowing that the flight would require special supervision and attention due to the medical issues that had afflicted the Professor. His disease had left him without the use of his arms, legs or voice—though he was able to articulate through a specially-designed computer interface that included vocal output that 'read' the words he dictated via the eye-controlled PC.

"As someone who has studied gravity and black holes all of my life, I am excited to experience first-hand weightlessness and a Zero-Gravity environment," Hawking said. "I am thankful to Zero-Gravity for making this experience available to the general public, especially for disabled individuals."

"The key thing here is that weightless and personal spaceflight is something available to everyone, even someone like Prof. Hawking," noted Peter Diamandis. "This is something that almost everyone can now experience."

It was an awesome plan… but the reality was far more intense.

Toward the end of the day of that triumphant flight, while driving back from the Shuttle Landing Facility aboard a NASA crew bus, I watched that amazing man form his first cohesive words, following a triumphant, albeit temporary, release from the clutches of gravity...

I... T...

W... A... S...

A... M... A... Z... I... N... G...

Those were the first words laboriously dictated to his computer system by famed scientist, astrophysicist, researcher and educator Stephen Hawking. In the accompanying words and pictures, let me share with you some of the background, details, and sensations I noted during a truly amazing day while serving as Zero-G's photographer aboard G-Force One... one that I think will be prominent in my memories for a long time. I've done this many times... but this time, well, it was special.

And yes... it was, indeed, amazing. Absolutely.

Under the expert and exhaustive supervision of XPrize and Zero-G founder, Dr. Peter Diamandis, every aspect of the "Hawking Flight" was practiced the day before, including a full dress rehearsal flight, until we felt that nothing was left to chance... As it turned out, the prep was a bit of overkill, as the flight went off superbly and without a glitch.

On board "G-Force One," dozens of Hawking fans, friends and support staff made ready to enjoy the Professor's release from terrestrial gravity. The energy level was high and spirits were (literally) soaring.

This was a full flight... filled with Zero-G staffers, Hawking's staff, some medical personnel (there to monitor the Professor and collect data for future flights involving the disabled), and a few folks that bid big dollars to several worthy charities in order to be observers to a unique 'moment in time.'

Hawking caregiver Monica Guy, Nicola O'Brien and Peter Diamandis (who, by the way, is also an MD) settled in quickly with Doctor Hawking and made sure that he was prepared well for the more 'weighty' aspects of the flight.

Professor Hawking was monitored carefully by an amiable and professional staff of medical specialists, who obviously bonded strongly with him and were quite attentive to every aspect of his needs. Interestingly; Hawking's vital stats changed very little during the flight. Positioned near some of the instrumentation, I can verify that Hawking's heart rate varied little between the positive and Zero-G excursions of the flight—and his smile showed that he was having the time of his life.

No kidding, the professor was all smiles throughout the flight and kept signaling to his caregivers that he wanted to do more parabolas as each one was completed... they were hoping to do one... they did eight!

Shuttle Astronaut/Scientist Byron Lichtenberg and Peter Diamandis carefully monitored Hawking throughout the Zero-G maneuvers, lifting him as the "G" dissipated, and then letting him fly free of gravity, and his wheelchair, for the first time in decades. As gravity came off, his smile deepened, his eyes twinkled and much of the ravages of time and disease fell away.

No kidding... at this point I was crying all over the back of my camera.

I admit it. I wasn't the only one.

Peter got the crazy idea (many of which come naturally to him, with great frequency) of floating an apple alongside Doctor Hawking... in something of a tribute to Sir Isaac Newton... who might have gotten a chuckle out of the whole thing, we imagine.

Prof. Hawking's best-selling books, *A Brief History of Time* and *Black Holes and Baby Universes and Other Essays* examines the basic laws, history and future of the universe. Hawking is known for his contributions to the fields of cosmology and quantum gravity, especially in the context of black holes. He has also made public his interest in experiencing weightlessness, and the importance of space as the next frontier for human population. Next, Hawking wants to fly aboard SpaceShipTwo.

I hereby volunteer my services as the photographer for that mission.

Hawking's staff and caregivers were elated... they obviously cared deeply for him.

The one good idea that I'll lay claim to was my suggestion to Peter that all the flyers and support staff line both sides of Hawking's exit, as he emerged, triumphantly, from G-Force One... to applaud his spirit, his courage and his vision... and yeah... again, there wasn't a dry eye on the ramp.

As he came back to earth, we applauded and celebrated his triumph with deep and genuine enthusiasm.

"Professor Hawking's expression said it all—the grins of sheer joy and excitement he displayed were unmistakable and no different than the giddiness and fun that all of our flyers experience," noted Peter Diamandis. "For me personally, and for all of us at Zero-G, it has been a complete honor and thrill to give Professor Hawking this opportunity to fulfill one of his lifelong dreams."

I've been a part of many historic events in the aviation and aerospace world... but I can't imagine a single event that has been as emotionally and spiritually satisfying as what I was just a part of.

I FLEW with Stephen Hawking. Imagine that...

Space is a dream to many... even to those with disabilities and impediments that may, once, have kept them from fully believing that they could journey to the heavens and beyond. But Hawking went beyond all that... freed from a wheelchair, disease, and gravity; Astrophysicist/Gifted Human Being/Teacher/Professor Stephen Hawking flew... and flew well.

I know he wants to fly again.

Stephen Hawking Flies Free Aboard G-Force One in 2007

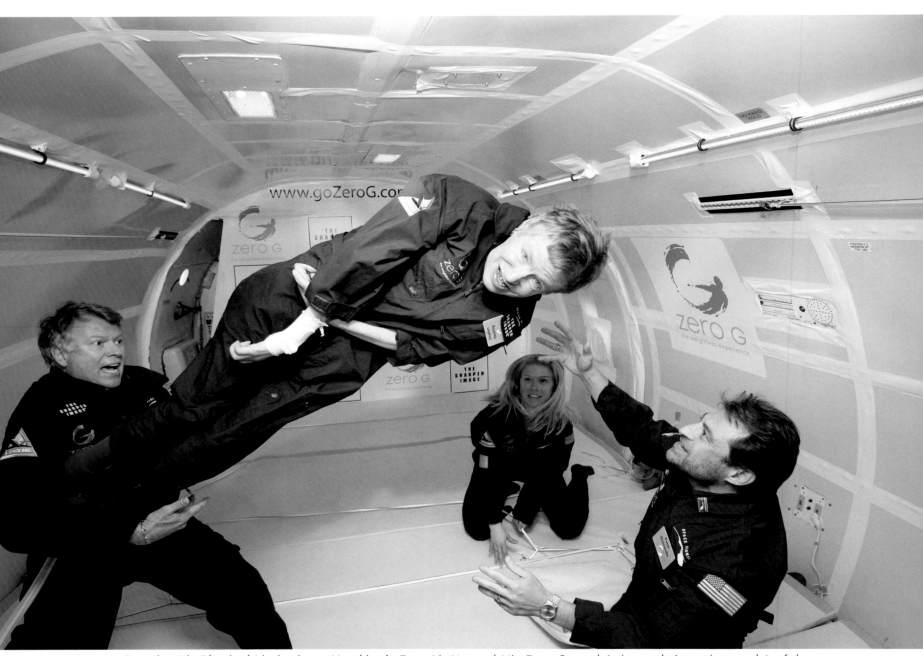

Despite His Physical Limitations, Hawking's Eyes Lit Up and His Face Stayed Animated, Attentive, and Joyful Throughout the Extended Flight

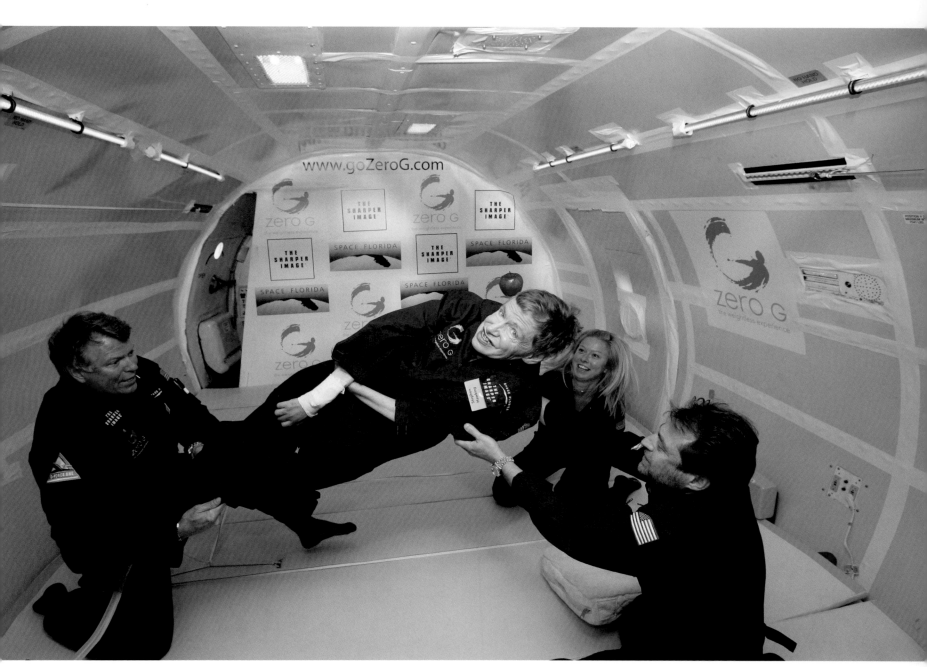

With a Free-Flying Apple (In Homage to Sir Isaac Newton), Hawking Was All Smiles

“I believe that life on Earth is at an ever-increasing risk of being wiped out by a disaster such as sudden nuclear war, a genetically engineered virus, or other dangers. I think the human race has no future if it doesn't go into space…”

—Dr. Stephen Hawking

"It was amazing. The Zero-G part was wonderful, and the high-G part was no problem. I could have gone on and on. Space, here I come."

—Dr. Stephen Hawking

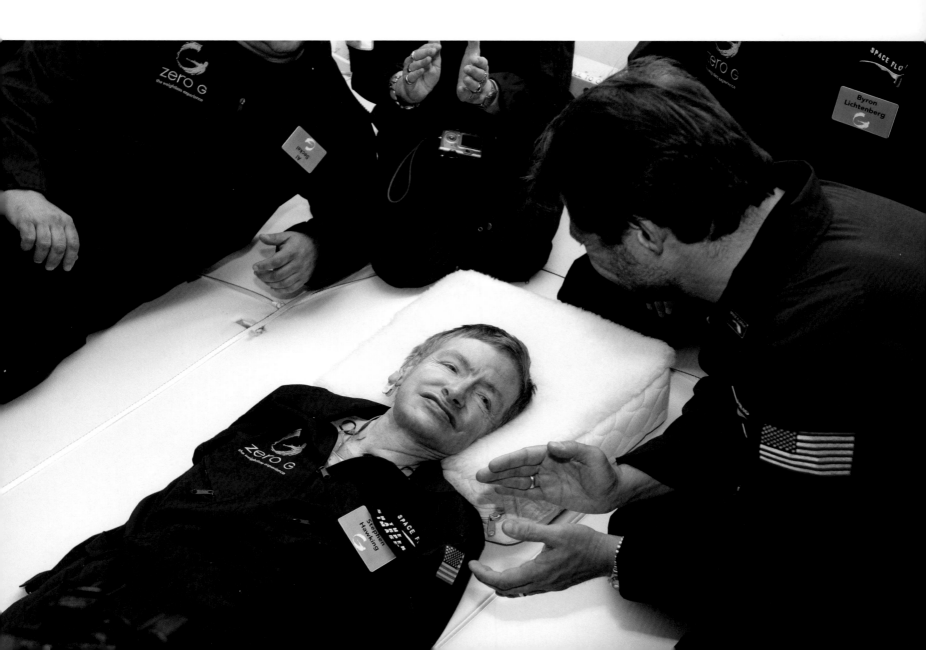

"We had a wonderful time. It was incredible, far beyond our expectations...
The doctors felt he was in tremendous condition. His heart rate, blood
pressure, oxygen levels were all normal and perfect..."

—Dr. Peter H. Diamandis, Chairman and CEO of the XPRIZE Foundation

The Atmosphere on Board G-Force One Was Ebullient… Everyone Knew That Something Remarkable Was at Hand

A Dedicated Medical Team Monitored Hawking Throughout the Flight, Both to Attend to His Health, as Well as to Capture Vital Data About the Effects of Zero-G

XPRIZE Cup: A Gathering Of The Space Family

Just imagine what a county fair would be like and feel like… if it was designed by Neil Armstrong. Or better yet, for those of you who have some familiarity with the aviation world, imagine an "Oshkosh for the space age."

Imagine that, and you may have some idea about what the XPRIZE Cup was all about. While the inaugural events were only presented across a handful of years, they were an inspiration to those of us who wanted to not only immerse ourselves in the present day wonders of the Personal Spaceflight revolution… but to also surround ourselves with the kind of people who could appreciate it as much as we did.

The events were as notable for their fellowship as they were for their demonstrations of an empowered future—XPRIZE-style.

And I have a feeling that as the XPRIZE revolution takes a greater part in all our lives, a new and greater XPRIZE Cup can't be all that far off in the future.

When first conceived, the inaugural event was, as noted, to be the Oshkosh of the space age. It was

meant to be an event, "where the average person can come and watch the next generations of space vehicles fly, where they can talk to the astronauts, see the vehicles up close, learn about the technology, and begin to dissolve the myth that they will never travel to space in their lifetime."

The original dream was aggressive… Intended to be hosted in Las Cruces, New Mexico for ten days each year, the XPRIZE Cup was expected to have even more amazing sights than the XPRIZE had brought forth up til that point...

Eventual iterations of the Cup were to offer competitive launch events in at least five categories:

- Fastest recycle time between the first launch and second landing,
- Maximum number of passengers per launch,
- Total number of passengers during the course of the competition,
- The maximum altitude achieved
- And the fastest flight time.

The XPRIZE Cup is designed to be an annual event in the spirit of the largest action-packed spectator events such as Grand Prix Racing and The America's Cup—but like all things that are so visionary, there is a time and a place for them... and for the funding necessary to see them through to completion.

Early offerings showed the best and brightest of the private space age... but were complex, expensive events to undertake... and only a few such events took place before the ravages of funding forced their halt... for now.

Still; they presented an up-close and personal viewpoint for tens of thousands of people to see the first public flights of the early Rocket Racers, numerous robotic rocket vehicles, dozens of small and medium rockets and on-site launches, and all manner of classes, forums, exhibits and displays. And while none of these events ultimately produced the financial results necessary to keep them running year after year, the visible impact on the faces of the thousands of men, women and kids that attended were beyond question.

The XPRIZE Cup was an inspiration to all in attendance.

Tens of thousands of people were taken to new heights as the new pioneers of the commercial space age conducted test-flights, engine firings, aircraft fly-ins and much more.

Pivotal among these were the first major demonstration flights of the Rocket Racing League's prototype 'EZ-Rocket'—a vehicle that trail-blazed the way for several more generations of exciting rocket-powered aircraft that were intended to be the start of a new series of space-age racing vehicles.

A product of the infinitely talented brains of XCOR Aerospace, the EZ-Rocket was the forerunner of the Rocket Racing League's Mark I racers. The EZ-Rocket last flew for the public in 2002 and the flights conducted at the XPRIZE Cup were dramatic,

numerous and breath-taking—and innovative. While the vehicle had flown a number of times in previous years, the XCOR team found the tasks ahead of them, as they refueled and readied the EZ-Rocket for multiple flights over the course of just a few days to be instructive, and at times, challenging.

But then again, as XCOR Boss Jeff Greason noted, "This really is rocket science!"

Another pivotal player in the XPRIZE Cup events were actual XPRIZE competitions like the Northrop Grumman Lunar Challenge—which in 2006 wound up with only one competitive entry that fielded two vehicles to the delight of thousands of avid spectators. Taking on the challenge, for the first time, was John Carmack's truly magnificent Armadillo Aerospace team... with their two robotic rockets — one named Texel and the other, Pixel...

As the accompanying photos show, there were a number of launch attempts, lots of great flying, and some truly expert work done in order to pursue this lofty goal... but the final flight, the one that would have earned Armadillo a first tier prize, was frustrated when minor damage done in the previous landing caused a series of events that initiated an inflight abort when the vehicle banked too aggressively shortly after liftoff, and the vehicle went down, damaging itself beyond the ability to fly again. It also provided one of those rare moments (albeit occasionally required) for those closely monitoring and participating in rocket research... the need to RUN!

As one of the team allowed in close proximity (thousands of feet away from the public areas) to the flying vehicles (as the event photographer), I found that when a vehicle like this starts to head off course and take a dive, its best to head for cover.

And we did—with no ill effect but a few breathless moments...

Other players in the nascent commercial space industry participated in many ways in these extraordinary gatherings… such as a number of the teams and vehicles that had contended for the XPRIZE itself as well as NASA, military, and civilian entrants.

And, yes, while the XPRIZE Cup events only managed to produce a few iterations, the blueprint they pioneered for future space-age gatherings and 'space-county fairs' remains an impressive starting point for the next generation of such events… which we predict are not too far off into the future.

We'll be there… and hope to see you there, too.

Armadillo Aerospace's 'Pixel' in a Challenge Flight at The XPRIZE Cup in 2006

At the 2006 XPRIZE Cup, There Was No Lack of Rocket Launches and Flights

"There are plenty of technology problems that must be faced... Technical problems only submit when they've been beaten to submission. And a lot of them are biting back."

—John Carmack, Armadillo Aerospace

"These guys are mavericks, just sitting on the edge of science and business. They're lean, they're flexible and they're very smart."

—XPRIZE Foundation Spokesperson, Ian Murphy

The Extraordinary Anousheh Ansari Signs One of Many Autographs for a Wide-Eyed Child... She LOVED Doing This

Prepping for a Rocket Launch at the XPRIZE CUP in 2006... No Matter the Size of the Vehicle, the Rocket Crews Took These Events VERY Seriously

WHOOOOOSH! Another XPC Launch Thrills the Thousands That Attended the 2006 XPRIZE Cup

Above: Buzz Aldrin Holds Court… a Major XPRIZE Proponent, the Media Paid Attention to the Moon-Walker's Every Word

A Major Crowd-Pleaser, the Flights of Rocketman Dan Schlund Were a Solid Highlight of the 2006 XPRIZE Cup

Armadillo Aerospace Prepares Its Robotic Rocket for Another Competition Flight

Rocket Racing League:
Rocketmen, You Have A Race

The ever-imaginative folks behind XPRIZE were barely done (again) with one project before XP Boss Peter Diamandis and his good friend, Granger Whitelaw (twice an Indianapolis 500 champion team partner), prepared yet another surprise in 2006. Just like the lessons learned from the Orteig prize that inspired XPRIZE, Peter and his crew drew from the lessons of history, remembering well that the early years of air racing produced extraordinary leaps in aviation technology and airplane design… and decided to use that as a roadmap to create the Rocket Racing League.

And while I was used to being included in the latest and greatest of the XPRIZE bag of world-changing tricks, this time I was going to go 'all-in.'

And it started in the usual way… with an email from Peter.

When Peter emails me, I pay attention.

Nothing dull ever happens around him, and the past few years or so of our friendship had proven that quite dramatically. Hanging with Peter is like trying to ride a roller coaster without a seat-belt… but with a lot more twisting and turning—and is a hell of a LOT more fun. He's one of the genuine souls that proves Ernest Hemingway's dictum that, "As you get older it is harder to have heroes, but it is sort of necessary."

And that one message from Peter, though, proved to be one of the most interesting of my life.

All it said was…

"Zoom, you're going to be a Rocket Racer."

What I had been drafted into (albeit quite willingly) was none other than the (then) soon-to-be-announced Rocket Racing League. The futuristic league was conceived to be an aerospace entertainment organization that combined the competition of racing with the space-age excitement of rocketry.

Similar to auto racing organizations, the RRL set out to organize, host and run competitions across the United States, with the finals to take place each year at the XPRIZE Cup in New Mexico. The league also planned to produce nationwide tours of its rocket planes and pilots to answer the public's demand for high-excitement entertainment. A video game based on the RRL was also being designed to allow the public to get intensely involved with the space-age startup—even to 'fly along' with racers in real-time.

Initial expectations (which rapidly evolved) expected that Rocket Races were to operate much like auto races, with the primary exception that the 'track' would be aloft, in the sky. Courses were initially expected to be approximately two miles long, one mile wide, and about 5,000 feet high, running perpendicularly to spectators. The rocket planes, called X-Racers, would take off from a runway either in a staggered fashion and side-by side and fly a course based on the design of a Grand Prix competition, with long straight-aways, vertical ascents, and deep banks. Each pilot would follow his or her own virtual 'tunnel' or 'track' of space through which to fly, safely separated from their competitors by several hundred feet.

Upon take-off, onlookers would follow the race as the rocket planes remained in view and sport 20' rocket plumes (with the rocket exhaust augmented, chemically, to produce a BRIGHT THICK discharge). Fans were also to be enabled to track their favorite pilots' progress via large screen televisions and hand-held GPS tracking devices using WiFi to stream video of the cockpit, live 'on-track' shots, 'side by side' views and wing angle views.

In the meantime, fans at home would have access to a three-dimensional course following the same 'tracks' the Rocket racers would be following for real. Special effects for lap completions, barrier violations and penalties would also be a part of the show.

There was much more… and the project advanced rapidly as both the technology and the excitement accelerated. Four Founding Pilots were selected to guide the early genesis of the program: Shuttle Veteran Colonel Rick Searfoss, Airshow Pilot Sean D. Tucker, XPRIZE's Erik Lindbergh (Grandson of Charles!) and Test Pilot/Aviation Journalist Jim Campbell (a.k.a. yours truly, the guy who wrote this book in your hands… yup… ME!).

Wow…

Joining this group was heady stuff… we were already all good friends—we knew (pretty much) what we were getting into… and the future looked amazing.

But, damn it, the future also looked really difficult.

RRL chose to take on not just one, but dozens, of challenges (and complex technologies) in this program… and over the course of nearly a decade of development, with the help of XCOR and Armadillo Aerospace (among others), several prototypes and generations of RocketPlane were developed and flown, a number of public demonstrations were conducted, and even a few formation flights were made with two vehicles flying at the same time. But… with the tanking of the economy, a severe drought in the availability of development and seed money, and a few political problems (that ate up a bit of time and resources), the Rocket Racing League remains a program with much potential… though much of it is, as yet, unrealized.

Mind you, the progress the program made was spectacular, and I have little doubt that not only will the program find a way to be a success at some point in our future… I still plan to do my best to be a part of it. Like the funding issues that killed many a promising aerospace venture, the Rocket Racing League needed lots of Bucks…

…And you gotta have the bucks if you want to play Buck Rogers.

I noted one thing early on during my public efforts as a member of the Rocket Racing League… this baby excited imaginations. Kids, adults, pilots, accountants, politicians, janitors… it didn't matter… EVERYONE wanted to be a Rocket Racer. The con-

An Early Prototype Rocker Racer Demonstrates Its Abilities at the XPRIZE Cup

cept was pure genius… and it excited people to no end.

Myself included.

Mind you… I've flown far more sophisticated flying machines well beyond the speed of sound and in regimes and conditions that made the early generation Rocket Racers look and sound meek by comparison… but the unbridled concept of rockets racing through the sky, while the rest of the world looked on in awe, just had a hook that dragged you in and would NOT let you go.

Getting named to this program was not, exactly, what I expected.

Instead of the ego boost one might assume one would get from such a selection, I was struck by the awesome opportunities ahead of me, the phenomenal responsibility I'd taken on, and the humbling reality of what lay ahead—but most prominent of all, were the thoughts of who I might inspire to seek their own challenges… in the sky, in space, and elsewhere.

As I am well aware of the pinnacle events that have inspired me to live the life I've made for myself… I wanted, very very much, to provide similar incentives to a potential fellow rocketeer.

So… Inspiration is important to me.

For instance, there is a lovely recurrent memory that comes to me when it can fight its way through all the detritus that clogs my cluttered cranium. Not so very long ago (or so I keep telling myself...), I perused the library shelves of the Brinkerhoff Elementary School in search of Robert Heinlein's latest Sci-Fi books in order to partake in a feverish dream that was just getting a toehold on my soul as I was working my way through second grade. The dream had been growing within me since I was old enough to understand the allure of the sky. *Rocket-Ship Galileo, Have Space Suit-Will Travel, The Man Who Sold The Moon* and so many other works of inspired genius became favored texts and the source of many a daydream and somehow, through it all, I was inspired to believe that I might someday fly aboard a rocket… and when you're all of seven or eight years old, there is not a doubt in your mind that all things are possible.

I remember it all so clearly... the feel of the dust cover, the smell of all the books—old and new—in the library, the weight of each volume in my hand, and the delicious anticipation I'd feel for those moments in which I'd finally sit down to read and journey off to galaxies of stunning imagination and great daring.

I just knew my life was to be full of such things.

I just knew it.

Because to a child, there are nothing but possi-

As a Preview of the Rocket Racing League, XCOR's EZ-Rocket Lights Off One of Its Two Engines on a Low Pass

Two Burning! The EZ-Rocket Takes Off at the XPRIZE Cup

bilities. And the XPRIZE was simply the most inspirational program I'd ever encountered—with more possibilities than any I'd ever worked with.

It is the process of maturing that brings the more disappointing aspects of reality to the fore, leaving many of us to forget the treasured joys of imagining great things and seemingly improbable futures. Because of the way that I was raised and the examples set before me by some amazing people (my family, most of all), I rarely lost sight of the fact that most all things were possible to those who were willing to strive for them.

That's one of the reasons that I so enjoy people like Peter, Granger, and the XPRIZE gang... as they are folks who also grew up believing in their ability, even

their right, to do and be a part of great things, even so-called 'impossible' things—and have never lost sight of that.

These are worthy people with which to surround yourself—and brilliant, if improbable, challenges like the Rocket Racing League inspire us all to seek heights barely dreamed of—and allow us to inspire the next generation that will far exceed our best efforts. RRL had the most exciting potential, of all things possible, in the RRL program... and it is why I believe that this is a dream that will come true.

So... someday, somewhere, do not be surprised to see me on the Rocket Racing circuit... I'll be the guy in the lead, having the time of my life... I swear.

"My dad told me that it was OK with him if I went into the rocket business. As long as I understood I was going to be poor."

—XCOR's Rich Pournelle.

"Yeah…. It's EVERY bit as fun as it looks."

—XCOR Pilot/Former Astronaut Col. Rick Searfoss, USAF (ret).

Purging the Propulsion System, Pilot Rick Searfoss Gets Ready for an XPC Flight

"I think people get excited about space again when they think some day they might get to go... Exploration is a lot more interesting when you think some day you and your kids might get to go see those places that are being explored."

—XCOR CEO Jeff Greason

"We've made great strides... we are looking forward to getting to racing and exhibiting a 21st century sport for the 21st century sports fan."

—Rocket Racing League Founding CEO Granger Whitelaw

Pilot Rick Searfoss and Rocket Racing League Boss, Granger Whitelaw

"The Rocket Racing League will inspire people of all ages to once again look up into the sky to find inspiration and excitement. New aerospace technologies coupled with the spirit of competition will not only extend the boundaries of entertainment, but continue the public's appetite for space ignited a year ago when the Ansari X PRIZE was awarded."

—Dr. Peter H. Diamandis, Chairman and Co-founder of the Rocket Racing League

"I noted one thing early on during my public efforts as a member of the Rocket Racing League… this baby excited imaginations. Kids, adults, pilots, accountants, politicians, janitors… it didn't matter… EVERYONE wanted to be a Rocket Racer. The concept was pure genius… and it excited people to no end. Myself included."

—One of the Four Founding Rocket Racing League Pilots, Jim Campbell

Aloft Over New Mexico, Thousands Witnessed the Public XPC Flights of the EZ-Rocket

At the Oshkosh/AirVenture Fly-in, In 2008, a More Advanced Rocket Racer Prototype Preps for an Exciting Public Demonstration at the Largest Aviation Event in the World

A Test Firing on the Main Runway at Oshkosh... Pure Rocket Power!

*The Unveiling of the Pilots and Management Team
of the Rocket Racing League, in NYC, 2005*

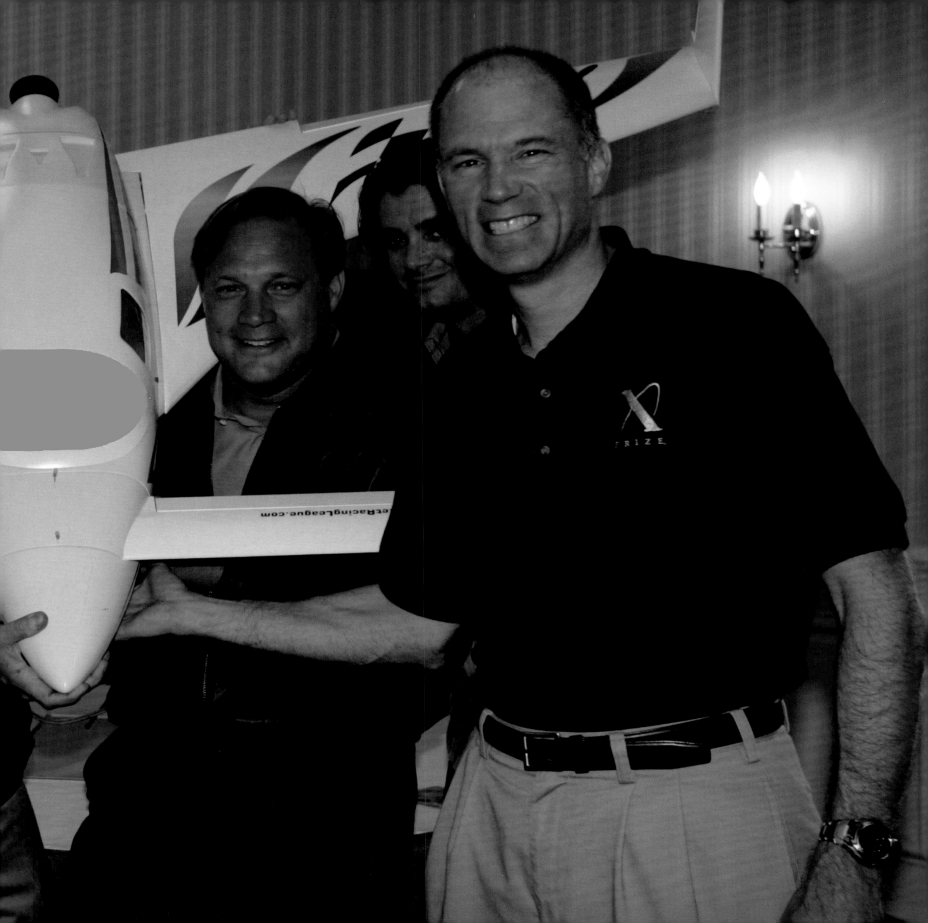

Peter Diamandis, Swarmed by Media after the Announcement Establishing the

The Google Lunar XPrize: Getting Back To What Neil And Buzz Started

Competition. Challenge. Innovation.

These concepts are the very essence of the XPRIZE.

So, it did not take long for the fertile minds of the XP team to come up with a new prize once SpaceShipOne had created a glorious new future… one that literally traversed space from world to world. It also produced a partnership that was destined to propel all things XPRIZE into even greater notoriety than ever before.

In the fall of 2007, The XPRIZE Foundation and Google announced the Google Lunar XPRIZE, a robotic race to the Moon to win a $30 million prize purse. Private companies from around the world were invited to compete to land a privately funded robotic rover on the Moon that was capable of completing several mission objectives, including roaming the lunar surface for at least 500 meters and sending video, images and data back to the Earth.

"The Google Lunar XPRIZE calls on entrepreneurs, engineers and visionaries from around the world to return us to the lunar surface and explore this environment for the benefit of all humanity," said Dr. Peter H. Diamandis, Chairman and CEO of the XPRIZE Foundation.

"We are confident that teams from around the world will help develop new robotic and virtual presence technology, which will dramatically reduce the cost of space exploration."

"Having Google fund the purse and title the competition punctuates our desire for breakthrough approaches and global participation," continued Diamandis. "By working with the Google team, we look forward to bringing this historic private space race into every home and classroom. We hope to ignite the imagination of children around the world."

In the 1960s, the United States and the Soviet Union engaged in a historic superpower Moon race, which culminated in 12 men exploring the surface of the Moon. The first era of lunar exploration reached a dramatic conclusion in December 1972, as Apollo 17

Peter Diamandis Explains the Stunning Mission of the Google Lunar XPRIZE

Astronauts Captain Gene Cernan and Dr. Harrison Schmitt became the last men to walk on the Moon.

In the nearly 40 years since Neil and Buzz had walked on the moon, it escaped NO ONE's notice that none had followed the crew of Apollo 17... and that steps like the Google Lunar XPRIZE might be just what it took to jump-start a new race back to the moon.

As originally conceived (and updated since the original announcement in 2007), the $30 million Prize purse was segmented into a $20 million Grand Prize, a $5 million Second Prize and $5 million in bonus Prizes. To win the Grand Prize, a team must successfully soft land a privately funded spacecraft on the Moon, rove on the lunar surface for a minimum of 500 meters, and transmit a specific set of video, images and data back to the Earth.

The Grand Prize was $20 million until December 31, 2012; thereafter it was intended to drop to $15 million until December 31, 2014 at which point the competition will be terminated unless extended by Google and the XPRIZE Foundation (which has since been extended until December 31, 2015).

To win the Second Prize, a team must land their spacecraft on the Moon, rove and transmit data back to Earth. Second place will be available until December 31, 2014 at which point the competition will be terminated unless extended by Google and the XPrize Foundation (which has also since been extended until December 31, 2015).

Bonus Prizes can be won by successfully completing additional mission tasks such as roving longer distances (less than 5,000 meters), imaging man-made artifacts (e.g. Apollo hardware), discovering water ice, and/or surviving through a frigid lunar night (approximately 14.5 Earth days). The competing lunar spacecraft are required to be equipped with high-definition video and still cameras, with which they will send images and data to Earth, which the public will be able to view on the Google Lunar XPRIZE website.

In 2013, XPRIZE and Google announced a supplemental series of Milestone Prizes that, "allow competing teams to access portions of the total prize purse as substantial technical achievements are achieved. The Milestone Prizes were added to recognize the technological achievements and the associated financial hurdles faced by the teams as they prepare their lunar spacecraft. A team can win Milestone Prizes for developing space hardware, launching their vehicle, or reaching a certain distance from the lunar surface. The money awarded as Milestone Prizes will be deducted from the grand prize or second place prize."

Activity, in mid-2014, remains aggressive, intense and on-going... with launch attempts now expected in the next year or so—and get this, the whole thing will become its own reality series. History will be seen and made in real-time.

At this point; the XPRIZE revolution seems ready to make its first leap off the planet, itself... and from there, it's anyone's guess as to how far the pioneering spirit of the XPRIZE will take us all.

XPRIZE's Robert Weiss Explains the Complex Mission Each GLXP Contender Will Have to Undertake

"The Google Lunar XPrize calls on entrepreneurs, engineers and visionaries from around the world to return us to the lunar surface and explore this environment for the benefit of all humanity. We are confident that teams from around the world will help develop new robotic and virtual presence technology, which will dramatically reduce the cost of space exploration."

—Dr. Peter H. Diamandis, Chairman and CEO of the XPRIZE Foundation

Buzz Aldrin Was Pleased to See a Potential Return to the Moon and Spoke Passionately About the Importance of Lunar Exploration

Google Committed Over $30 Million to Seek Our Return to the Moon

Where Do We Go From Here?

Ten years… don't they go by in a flash?

And yet, as consequential and innovative as this past decade has been, I have a feeling that the next could eclipse it all by quite a bit… and I pray that this comes to pass. Like many things in the aviation and aerospace world, our rate of evolution has slowed… and the most powerful enemy of progress in the aero-world is the phrase… "Well, that's the way we've always done it."

That was… until XPRIZE cast such aphorisms aside and convinced the world that radical and innovative change, competitively provoked, could better the world around us in so many ways. And that's just what XPRIZE has done… and not just for our beloved space and aviation industries, but across a number of difficult disciplines—automotive, genomics, medicine, oceaneering, environmental, education, robotics and so much more.

Buzz Aldrin tells me that all revolutions start with the smallest of steps (and he should know)—the germ of an idea—and then another—and another—until a series of evolutionary improvements produces the cascade effect that creates a true revolution. Via this book, I've been privileged to share with you some amazing sights and stories. I've told you about a few

revolutions that I was privileged to be a part of, in the past, and will continue to be a part of in the future.

And yet… as I read this… as I revisit the memories, the pictures, the notes and the data, I am alarmed to feel a little too much satisfaction… and not nearly enough zeal to venture even further and farther than I have over this past decade… and ultimately, that's a really good and valuable thing. Yeah; it's time to step up my game… to push harder and more deliberately toward the better future that we deserve.

Why?

Because those who stand still, mesmerized by their so-called successes, are bound to be run over by those who are rushing forward to build an altogether new future… even a radical one. It's 'innovation' pure and simple, Innovation 101, if you will. Evolutionary changes build upon one another until the resultant cascade effect creates true Transformation, lasting revolution, sustainable industries and a new future for the world…

But you can't stop and enjoy the successes (or lick your wounds over your failures), simply because progress requires movement and direction and energy—hence, the message and lessons inherent in all things XPRIZE and the amazing little inside secret of it all is this—The True Value of the XPRIZE was not just in what it produced, but the many ways it mobilized thousands, even tens of thousands, of people to affect our futures in the most positive, and progressive manner possible. There is no revolution without the requisite number of revolutionaries— like the visionaries who created XPRIZE and the

thousands of people who played their part in this magnificent decade.

So… where do we go from here?

Straight on to the future—one that is likely to be more exciting and capable than we dreamed, and might be far more positive then we dreamed of.

Just follow the path of the XPRIZE…